Gendered Power

MICHIGAN MONOGRAPH SERIES IN JAPANESE STUDIES

NUMBER 86

CENTER FOR JAPANESE STUDIES
UNIVERSITY OF MICHIGAN

Gendered Power

EDUCATED WOMEN OF THE MEIJI EMPRESS' COURT

Mamiko C. Suzuki

UNIVERSITY OF MICHIGAN PRESS
ANN ARBOR

Published in the United States of America by the
University of Michigan Press
Printed and bound by CPI Group (UK) Ltd, Croydon, CR0 4YY

First published January 2019

A CIP catalog record for this book is available from the British Library.

Library of Congress Cataloging-in-Publication Data

Names: Suzuki, Mamiko C., author.
Title: Gendered power : educated women of the Meiji Empress' court / Mamiko C. Suzuki.
Description: Ann Arbor : University of Michigan Press, [2019] | Series: Center for Japanese
    Studies monograph series | Includes bibliographical references. |Identifiers: LCCN
    2018040650 (print) | LCCN 2018058831 (ebook) | ISBN 9780472124169 (E-book) |
    ISBN 9780472073979 (hbk : alk. paper) | ISBN 9780472053971 (pbk : alk. paper) |
    ISBN 9780472124169 (ebk)
Subjects: LCSH: Women intellectuals—Japan—History. | Women—Japan—Social
    conditions. | Women—Education—Japan—History. | Japan—Intellectual life—1868–
    | Shōoken, Empress, consort of Meiji, Emperor of Japan, 1850–1914. | Women and
    literature—Japan—History.
Classification: LCC HQ1762 (ebook) | LCC HQ1762 .S9725 2019 (print) |
    DDC 305.40952—dc23
LC record available at https://lccn.loc.gov/2018040650

For Akira, Kaoru, Hiromi, and Chaitanya

CONTENTS

Digital materials related to this title can be found on the Fulcrum platform via the following citable URL: https://doi.org/10.3998/mpub.9856453

ACKNOWLEDGMENTS

For the completion of this book I owe thanks to numerous friends, colleagues, and family members. I am deeply indebted to my dissertation committee. My chair, Norma Field, supported my scholarly development and inspired me to assert my voice as a student and as a researcher. Susan Burns urged me on in my exploration of Meiji gender issues and encouraged me to persevere as a scholar. Michael Bourdaghs was a generous advisor who provided invaluable insight and support. The courses I took with Tetsuo Najita and Bill Sibley prepared me to tackle Meiji-period materials.

I am also grateful to the late professor Kan Satoko at Ochanomizu University, who provided unwavering enthusiasm and shared generously of her extensive knowledge of Meiji women's writing. I owe much also to Professors Sally Hastings, Margaret Mitsutani, Christine Marran, Rebecca Copeland, Tim van Compernolle, and Seki Reiko for paving the way for research in the writings of Meiji women and for advice and insight along the way. Harumi Sanpei helped me immensely in deciphering Shōen's *kanbunmyaku nikki*.

My research in Japan was made possible with grants from the Fulbright Commission, the Center for East Asian Studies, and the Japanese Committee at the University of Chicago. Subsequent research trips to Japan to collect materials at the National Diet Library, the Jissen University Shimoda Utako Archives, and the Imperial Household Public Archives were funded with a University of Utah University Research Committee's Faculty Research Fellowship, a Northeast Asia Council Japanese Studies Grant, and multiple University of Utah Asia Center Travel Grants and College of Humanities International Travel Grants.

Three anonymous readers were generous in their comments, and their suggestions helped to improve the project. I thank Christopher Dreyer, editor at the University of Michigan Press, for his encouragement and patience.

I am deeply indebted to fellow graduate students and to postdoctoral researchers at the University of Chicago: Nicholas Albertson, Brian Bergstrom, Heather Bowen-Struyk, Heekyoung Cho, Mika Endo, Fumiko Jōo, Anup Grewal, Patti Kameya, Hyun-jeong Lee, Jaeyon Lee, Tanya Maus, Scott Mehl, Miho Matsugu, Tomoko Seto, Katy Tanaka, Tomomi Yamaguchi, and many others whose encouragement, support, intellectual engagement, and example sustained me throughout my graduate career. Thanks also to my Chicago *senpai* Amanda Seaman, Alisa Freedman, and Sarah Frederick for their encouragement and advice.

At the University of Utah, I received an invaluable amount of support and mentorship from my colleagues Wesley Sasaki Uemura, Shoji Azuma, Richard Chi, Therese De Raedt, Tanya Flores, Eric Hutton, Yukio Kachi, Mimi Locher, Jia-Wen Guo, Li Guo (Utah State University), Joe Metz, David Roh, Lien Fan Shen, Cindi Textor, Janet Theiss, Margaret Wan, Margaret Toscano, and Fusheng Wu. I am grateful to all my colleagues in the World Languages and Cultures Department and to my department chair, Katharina Gerstenberger. I was fortunate to have wonderful students and friends in Salt Lake City and especially thank Haylen LaTorre, Seth Radford, Dale Strobel, and Yichu Su.

As this project developed, I enjoyed stimulating intellectual exchanges during my research year in Japan with Takeuchi Kayo, Satoko Naitō, and Abbie Yamamoto. I am deeply grateful to Robert Tuck for his advice on the *kanshi* translation and to Fumiko Jōo for her friendship and her guidance on the *kanshi* and *kanbun* translations.

This decades-long endeavor began in my undergraduate studies at Haverford College, where I was fortunate to receive encouragement and guidance from Matthew Mizenko, Ayako Kano (University of Pennsylvania), Carol Bernstein (Bryn Mawr College), and Julia Epstein.

I am grateful to numerous family members in Japan, whose kindness and generosity sustained my connection to Japan. I am especially indebted to the generosity and support of my aunts Michiko Tsuruta and Toshiko Usami. I am also grateful to Mortimer, Marlene, Miriam, Myrcene, and Frederick for their love.

Finally, I dedicate this book to Chaitanya, Hiromi, Kaoru, and Akira, whose love and support made every step possible.

INTRODUCTION

In the late nineteenth century, Japanese women strategized against the social and legal constraints that the Meiji imperial government (1868–1912) produced for its national education system. Women's responses to the limitations and contradictions that arose as Meiji gender roles transformed throughout this period are the main focus of this study. As the Meiji government sought to modernize, women were deemed essential to Japan's modernization process, and education was considered the key area in which to actively train, employ, and deploy women to build a strong nation. New hierarchies based on the acquisition of a modern education were designed and implemented separately for men and women and thus required women's inclusion in public roles. If women could master and apply modern concepts essential to nation building, they would be useful to the Meiji bureaucracy.[1] Although the promulgation of the Meiji Constitution in 1890 solidified the Meiji government's outright rejection of women's suffrage, education then emerged as the main arena in which to define how women should participate in a modern nation. That the Meiji decades from 1890 onward are more often understood as periods of increased repression, marginalization, and silencing of Japanese women obscures the fact that women were recruited and actively participated in modernizing Japan and were not restricted only to the role of housewives tending to the home.[2]

As Koyama Shizuko has argued, the ideology of *ryōsai kenbo* (good wife, wise mother) grew out of the debates over women's education and became the anchor by which the modern family was used as a major site of recruitment for female laborers.[3] *Ryōsai kenbo* is a concept that draws from traditional Confucian teachings but in fact was a modern ideal promoted by the Meiji government; Meiji-period philosopher Nakamura Masanao

(1832–91) first used the term in its modern rendition in 1891.[4] As a modern educational system was taking shape throughout the Meiji period, standards for the instruction of female students, which expanded upon the concept of *ryōsai kenbo*, and the socially accepted methods of women's public participation continually transformed. Competing models for girls' and women's education existed from early on in the Meiji period—schools opened by Christian missionaries trained students in English, while *kanbun juku* (private academies of Chinese learning) continued to teach classical Chinese into the late 1880s.

Those women who helped to shape the educational policies and curricula for girls in the mid-Meiji period shared several common resources: their ties to imperial authority, their classical Chinese proficiency, and their enthusiasm for educating women. These characteristics shaped the germination period of Meiji women's education as these women created female-centered sites of negotiation and action to achieve women's social importance. Those who spearheaded government-sponsored educational practices enjoyed close ties to Meiji bureaucracy and to the imperial court, but this did not mean that they simply followed received injunctions. In fact, their efforts to define modern Japanese womanhood were steeped in contradictions. The ideals of Meiji womanhood that emerged in the mid- to late Meiji period mirrored the complexities of the women who helped author them. Both old and new standards of ideal womanhood had to be negotiated as those entrusted with reform managed new forms of power and invented new feminine traditions.

It is important to emphasize that the expressions of Meiji women's power invoked in this study are distinct from the kinds of power held by male elites of the period. The main sources of gendered power held by Meiji women existed in the realms of education, domestic science, nursing, charitable organizations, and the international networks built upon these areas of interest. Their spheres of influence included schools, hospitals, and the imperial court. This study considers Meiji women's power to act within these realms and the paradoxes that emerged from the various exercises of that power. Naming their influence as a kind of power recognizes that, even in a socially subordinate role, women's actions and efforts were not without consequence.

The paradoxes of Meiji womanhood are evident in the ambiguity of women's ability and potential, particularly among those who benefited from the imperial government's support for modern women's education. Elite and influential Meiji women participated in what Takashi Fujitani calls the paradox of an emperor-centered nationalism that required "the imperial institution's new emergence in modern Japan."[5] Such women benefited from their ties to the imperial institution and came to embody the height of influence and ability to change social norms by shaping standards on a national scale. The following chapters demonstrate that the paradoxes faced particularly by elite and influential Meiji women were not characterized by powerlessness. In fact, when considered together with imperial authority, a different picture of female-centered power emerges. That picture illustrates the struggle between the Meiji women who continued to call for women's suffrage and openly rejected the ideals of marriage and motherhood promoted by the government and those who were at the forefront of such nationalizing and normalizing efforts—those with social and even political power.

The Spaces of Meiji Women's Power

Women's education produced contradictory effects, functioning both as a source of modern women's empowerment and as a means to supervise and monitor them. Meiji women's empowerment can also be mapped by competing definitions of womanhood, which were enacted in contradiction to stated aims in highly gendered spaces.[6] Focusing on empowerment allows us to reject the dyad of male master and female slave as insufficient to examine fully the gender dynamics of the Meiji era. Identifying instances of women's ability and power, even as they were subjected to male supremacy, enables us to closely examine the unsteady boundary negotiated by prominent women whose public roles rested on the reinvention of private roles for women but whose public legitimacy could be stripped away by the very rules they crafted.

One unanticipated source of Meiji women's empowerment came through knowledge of the Chinese classics (*kanbun*) and of classical Chinese poetry (*kanshi*), which provided some women with social, even political, capital in the early to mid-Meiji period. The high level of education that *kanbun* proficiency (including the ability to read classical Chinese text to have knowledge of the Chinese classics) signified may have marked women as masculine, but it also provided a select few with professional employment, as highly educated women were recruited to serve the Meiji empress Haruko's (1849–1914) court. The imperial court was a new destination for highly educated women, a place of employment, an opportunity for social advancement, and at times an alternative to marriage. Women who passed through the imperial court and whose shared literacy in classical Chinese made them useful public servants acted as practitioners of court rituals, educators, translators, and cultural ambassadors for the Meiji government.

The Meiji empress, the preeminent bearer of Meiji gendered power, stood at the heart of a court of elite women and was a lifelong student of classical Chinese and Japanese. She is a crucial node within the early history of modern women's education. As an icon for the reforms that altered women's social status and educational opportunities, she and the elite women associated with her court worked within self-imposed definitions of feminine purpose and behavior. It is significant that she and others in her court also self-authored such standards of feminine behavior and that they were authorized to pursue their mission to educate and elevate the status of Japanese women as acts of national interest. Furthermore, the ideals that emerged from these women contributed to the vision of Japanese womanhood that was displayed and promoted to a newly interpolated population of female laborers, educators, housewives, and mothers.

The three main subjects of this study—Empress Haruko, Nakajima Shōen (1863–1901), and Shimoda Utako (1854–1936)—share a biographical detail: all three were childless and had complex connections to the ideal of motherhood that became the legitimating force behind Meiji women's importance to the nation. Thus their roles, which might be described as mothers of a new generation of women, are grounded in their work as social engineers of the ideas of motherhood and femininity. Childlessness was most problematic for Empress Haruko, whose inability to produce an heir almost led to her being unseated as empress by divorce but was resolved when the Meiji government and imperial advisors agreed to make the imperial couple's modern marriage monogamous only in ceremony. The empress was the emperor's ruling partner in all official capacities, thus heirs born of the emperor's concubines (*gon no tenji*) were adopted by the empress as her own children. While the Meiji emperor is widely viewed as the preeminent icon of Japan's modernization, art historian Wakakuwa Midori has pointed out that Empress Haruko was as essential an icon as the emperor, embodying an ideal womanhood and a maternal status without which a coherent view of the Japanese nation could not have emerged.[7] Especially in her public image and in the kinds of knowledge she promoted, she exemplified the paradoxical nature of the Meiji period that looked toward the future yet simultaneously referred back to ancient myth to establish legitimacy. In the empress' position as imperial monarch, her promotion of women's education counteracted widespread disdain for the education of women and assuaged fears that educated women would transgress the boundaries between private and public by participating in political activities. In short, her visibility and participation in civic duties were critical to Japan's national prominence among Western parliamentary monarchies. She was made an icon for the elevation of women's status in Japanese society and as such had lasting influence on the lives and identities of Japanese women and the empire as a whole.

The empress' authority enhanced the education-centered lives of Shōen and Utako, for both women were part of a new generation of court women due to their intellects rather than their aristocratic lineage. Both women had been educated in classical Chinese to a degree similar to men in learned households of the late Tokugawa to early Meiji eras—Shōen began her studies through the early Kyoto school system, and Utako received instruction from her Sinologist father. They shared with their male counterparts the difficulty of merging their classical Chinese education with the deluge of Western knowledge imported through both *kanbun* and English. Yet, as with other highly educated Meiji civil servants, it was this training that first equipped them to develop and execute the modernization of Japanese society, including the designing of modern education of future Japanese women.

Shōen would not live to participate in the late Meiji transformation of modern women's education, but she made early contributions as a writer, instructor, and commentator and drew from her classical Chinese training to promote education as a way to lead women to demand equal rights for themselves. The efforts that Utako and the Meiji empress made in the 1890s and 1900s to shape elite women's education reflect the complex gendered role that education played for women in the process of modernization. As a means to both exercise power and be subjected to it, Utako's career promoting gender-specific subjects can be seen as preventing women from attaining equality with men by subordinating their intellect to serve their families and, by extension, the nation-state.

The strategies that Utako and Shōen in particular used help us to clarify the distinctive power relationships that women in the Meiji period developed and sustained with each other. Utako and other contemporary educators of women—such as Miwada Masako, Atomi Kakei, and Tsuda Umeko—had the greatest influence in constructing and enforcing new norms for

women's education in Japan. Even as the spaces of modern women's education defined and monitored the bodies and thoughts of students, mothers,
teachers, and domestic and industrial workers, they also functioned as sites
of creative and strategic action. While such women located their power in its
enforcement rather than through resistance, the exercise of female empowerment in all its contradictions appears to us now less as masculine behavior
and more as strategic choices of modern women. The elite Meiji women who
constructed new models of womanhood through their work as educators
and writers were driven to improvise and adapt to changing conventions.

Meiji Women's Studies

Studies of extraordinary women from the late Tokugawa to early Meiji periods have filled key historical gaps, exploring the narratives of the lives and
ideas of educated Meiji women. Recent English-language scholarship by
Rebecca Copeland, Melanie Czarnecki, Christine Marran, Mara Patessio,
Marnie Anderson, and Elizabeth Dorn Lublin on Meiji women's writings,
education, and political activism has shed light on the collective emergence
of women in public spaces and their use of literary, social, and political
networks to support various national and local causes.[8] Meiji women were
expected to live domestic lives that supported an image of national health—
one that could be reinforced through public performance. In the case of
women who wrote, however, their published works allowed them to experience a degree of freedom and the opportunity to participate in public discourse, however narrow their influence.

There were relatively few venues in which these women could openly
express their views on the social restrictions placed on their writing and the
public monitoring of their behavior. None of the journals or newspapers of
the mid-Meiji period had female editors, and the few discursive sites that
accommodated women's speech were short-lived.[9] Hirata Yumi, for instance, describes how women were able to post their opinions in *koshinbun*
(little newspapers) during the 1870s. These publications were marketed toward less educated readers, specifically women and children, and set aside
sections for letters from women. These letters were published in the manner
of a discussion board and facilitated discursive exchanges between women
on a national scale. By the 1880s, however, the active participation of female
readers steeply declined as paid male columnists replaced readers' com-
ment sections, thereby suppressing women's voices.[10]

Scholarship on Meiji women has focused on writers who published alongside the famed Higuchi Ichiyō (1872–96) but were subsequently swept to the margins of literary history. Furthermore, as Rebecca Copeland has pointed out, the most visible female writers and activists of the Meiji period were highly vulnerable to the media's public examination of their private lives. Newspaper editorials, journal articles, and essays would reference female writers' private lives as often as they commented on their work.[11] Such surveillance of women's public expression was intended to manage their social behavior and thereby promote the well-being of the burgeoning nation.

In the areas of political discourse and popular rights, the historian Marnie Anderson has argued that the language of reform and feminine virtue existed within feminists' agenda in the Freedom and People's Rights Movement (Jiyū Minken Undō) of the 1880s and that the language of rights does not disappear entirely after 1890.[12] The mid-Meiji period also saw the emergence of women's associations, which were sizable organizations populated by women of the elite classes who supported Japan's military expansion abroad and its general development as a player on the international stage. Elizabeth Dorn Lublin examines the inner workings of one such group, the Woman's Christian Temperance Union, which successfully organized to influence popular opinion and social reform policies.[13] The flip side of the patriotic and noble bourgeois Japanese woman was the female deviant. Christine Marran has examined the subversive nature of the "poison woman," or *dokufu*, and the role that print media played in constructing distinctly female threats to a male-centered, normalized modern society.[14]

Much critical attention has been paid also to the political, social, and cultural strategies that produced a powerful imperial parliamentary system during the Meiji period and to *ryōsai kenbo* ideology's effects on the maternalization and domestication of women. Japanese feminist historians and literary scholars such as Kan Satoko, Kitada Sachie, Nishikawa Yūko, Ōki Motoko, Saeki Junko, Seki Reiko, and Sekiguchi Sumiko have produced a wealth of scholarship concerning the lives and writings of Meiji women, revealing Meiji women's discourses as constructed of a diverse array of writers and activists who challenged emerging norms for Meiji women. English-language scholars such as Sally Hastings, Margaret Mehl, Barbara Rose, and Martha Tocco have written of Meiji women's education and its prominent practitioners, such as Miwada and Tsuda. Their research has shown that Meiji women's education provided important opportunities for work and independent thought and allowed many women to achieve professional success. It is clear also that these achievements were often accomplished only through loopholes in a system that made it very difficult for other women to succeed on the public stage.

Drawing on this increased scholarly interest in women of the Meiji period, the present book considers the significance and influence of elite, educated Meiji women and their role in shaping the national identity of women in modern Japan. Carrying over these considerations both from previous English and Japanese scholarship, this study interrogates the political and cultural forces that positioned women as delegates of the Meiji empress' court or as exemplary Japanese women. It argues that the network of women emerging from the empress' court negotiated the visually, culturally, and educationally circulated feminine ideals and its effects that were carried out as components of a modern Japanese woman's identity.

Outline of Chapters

The first chapter of this book, "The Traditional and Modern Education of Empress Haruko and Her Court Women," analyzes Empress Haruko's role in shaping women's education as a training ground for patriotic and loyal women of the Japanese empire. It considers how practices central to the modernization of women's education flourished due to the patronage of the empress and provided women with the opportunity to be trained for professions that were suitable to women in their class. The empress financially supported various kinds of educational institutions for women, including elite schools that offered courses in classical literature as well as domestic science, and training schools for maids, seamstresses, and nurses. Women's literacy was encouraged as a necessary component of training women at all socioeconomic levels. While the empress' charitable efforts were modeled after those of Western female monarchs such as Queen Victoria of England (1819–1901) and Duchess Louise of Mecklenburg-Strelitz of Prussia (1776–1810), her enthusiastic sponsorship of girls' schools appeared sincere. Yet in the application of class-specific education, class divisions were reinforced, as poorer students received professional training after acquiring only basic reading and writing skills. Nevertheless, the curriculum at each of these girls' schools provided students with instruction and the possibility of enriching their own lives rather than only their future husbands' and children's lives. The limited applications for women's education in the mid- to late Meiji period did not make the schools themselves mere training grounds for housewives and mothers. The schools were one of the few but growing female-centered spaces in which the stated goal of training women for marriage and motherhood could not limit the degree of learning, community building, and identity formation that now existed as a women-only gathering site outside of the home.

At the heart of the politics and power at play among the elite women discussed in this book are the ideas of traditional education and of the traditional woman as they emerged in the Meiji period. I will argue that the combination of *kanbun* education and imperial rule in the guise of tradition worked to modernize women's education and the assumptions about womanhood promoted during this period.

The discursive space inhabited by popular rights activist Kishida Toshiko, who would later be known as Nakajima Shōen, is the focus of the second chapter, "From Kishida Toshiko to Nakajima Shōen: A Meiji Classical Chinese Foundation for a Modern Japanese Woman." The chapter examines how Shōen's classical Chinese education aided her in achieving fame as an orator in the early 1880s and allowed her to have a public presence as an educator, essayist, and poet in girls' schools and women's journals until her death in 1901. Shōen's writings can be divided into four categories: original and translated fiction; instructional and autobiographical essays, mostly published in the journal *Jogaku zasshi* (Journal for women's learning); her *kanshi*; and her diaries. Many studies of Shōen's career focus on her work with the Freedom and People's Rights Movement or her fictional works, neglecting her diaries and *kanshi* written near the end of her life, which reveal an outward-looking and informed perspective of a former orator and educator. Shōen's ill health and political setbacks led to relative seclusion in the later years of her life, leaving her to interact almost exclusively with members of her household but also through the written word. These texts demonstrate the tensions between her intellect and writing and the private discursive world she created out of newspapers, journals, and diary entries that became her main mode of engagement with the world. Her ostensibly private musings were expressive efforts to engage in a public discourse from which she had been sidelined due to her health and gender. Though she had been a political star in her own right, by 1890 she was playing a supporting role in the only feasible political career for anyone in her family, that of her husband Nobuyuki's run as the first Speaker of the lower house of the Diet. The deeply personal function of her *kanbunchō* (classical Chinese style of prose) diary became an outlet for her disappointed public ambitions, which included the elevation of women's status in Japan, and for the struggle against her deteriorating health.

Chapter 3, "Shimoda Utako and the Scandal of the Educated Female Body," examines both the official and the unauthorized reporting on Shimoda Utako, a woman who gained significant social influence through her prominent pedagogical work. Utako contributed to the construction of feminine national identity in the mid- to late Meiji period through her profession as an educator and as a national spokesperson for modern women's education. The media and populace held Utako to a distinct standard, expecting her to exemplify the norms she promoted because she was a leading educator of elite women and was a trusted servant of and advisor to the empress. As an educator, she promoted a utilitarian femininity that incorporated domestic skills but also offered artistic training for her female students. While presenting a dutifully feminine image, she carried out extraordinary tasks: traveling to Great Britain to collect educational materials and pedagogical techniques for women, for example, and producing numerous textbooks for female students on a variety of subjects, from classical Japanese literature to home nursing.

The greatest contradiction of Utako's career was revealed in the scandal that threatened to tarnish her reputation, a smear campaign carried out on the pages of the socialist newspaper *Heimin shinbun* (Commoners' newspaper), which challenged Utako's professional legitimacy by alleging illicit sexual relations and made her body a matter of public discussion. These tensions embodied modern women's access to power in which individual empowerment was matched against the interests of other, less powerful women. Despite this scandal, Utako continued to promote such ideals as the Old-Fashioned Woman (*furui onna*)—her response to the artistic awakening of the New Women of the Bluestockings coterie. Thus, in practice she executed new and unprecedented tasks for women yet was committed to a version of "old-fashioned" womanhood that allowed her to remain an influential educator of Japan's women.

By proposing and interrogating the possibility of Meiji women's power, the following chapters examine contradictions that were symptomatic of women's struggles within the vast social, cultural, and political transformations that took place during the Meiji period. An examination of that conflict within feminist history is crucial in order to understand what radical resistance meant in the face of women-centered authority.

A Note on Naming

All three of the women discussed in this book have multiple names that they used interchangeably at various points for distinct uses.

Kishida Toshiko was born Toshi, and her given name is most often associated with her days in the Freedom and People's Rights Movement. But Toshiko signed some of her early writings with Shun'nyo (a compound made up of the character for *toshi,* "outstanding," and woman). She signed her articles after 1884 with the pen name Shōen or also with the last name Nakajima, since most of her published writing appeared after her marriage to Nakajima Nobuyuki. Rather than refer to her by her husband's family name, I have opted to use her pen name, Shōen, especially since the materials discussed in chapter 2 refer to her diaries and poetry.[15]

Hirao Seki's name, Shimoda Utako, is also a combination of her husband's family name and a first name that was given to her upon a later date, in this case by Empress Haruko in recognition of her poetic talent. As Utako chose to officially accept this honor, she is referred to as Utako in chapter 3.

Empress Haruko's name was Ichijō Masako before marriage, and after Emperor Meiji's death it became Dowager Empress Shōken. In an effort to recognize the period of her life that is discussed in this book, I refer to her as Haruko or Empress Haruko.

CHAPTER 1

THE TRADITIONAL AND MODERN EDUCATION OF EMPRESS HARUKO AND HER COURT WOMEN

Introduction

The politics and power at play among Meiji elite women exist in the idea of traditional education and of the traditional woman as they emerged in the Meiji period. In particular, the combination of *kanbun* education and imperial rule worked to modernize women's education and the assumptions about womanhood. In this chapter I will first examine classical Chinese and Confucian educational materials promoted by Meiji imperial court advisors for their traditional content, which also could be applied to modern uses. Next, I will discuss how women who received this "traditional" yet, or therefore, modern education were given tasks and employment in the mid- to late Meiji period that placed them in unprecedented public positions, such as educators, journalists, and writers who were communicating with politicians and rulers. This is to show that while there was much that might be labeled traditional and conservative, new kinds of practices and social relationships were being forged in the imperial court and in the field of women's education. Finally, I will parse the role of Meiji empress Haruko, who embodied both the traditional and the modern, in order to shed light on the power of aristocratic privilege in the attainment of modern opportunities. By considering these overlapping Meiji constructions, I will examine the contradictions and privileges of Meiji elite women and the cost of power available to modern women. Women sought rights that required their recruitment into a still male-centered national cause that enabled some to become educated national subjects. In a variety of instances, they advanced their own roles and opportunities while narrowing those of others.

Kanbun Education as a Source of Power

Japanese feminist histories of the Meiji period have highlighted the emergence of women's political agency and at times presented the shift of attention to women's education as a lost opportunity and failure for the fight for women's political rights. But framing the movement for women's rights as in opposition to the movement for more women's education obscures how the modern advancements for women's status that were achieved throughout the twentieth century were based on strategies that would not resolve inequality among women. The realization of women's rights and education should be seen together with the degrees of privilege that were required to conceive of and implement greater social and political opportunities for all women. In fact, some would say the resources were available already to an elite few in the late Tokugawa period (ca.1700–1868). Only in the Meiji period were women identified as a group that could be harnessed to strengthen the nation. Thus, through education, women were socialized to contribute to the health and moral rigor of the nation by providing their fertility and domestic labor to their families. But in that socialization process, women also learned how to organize against social norms and behaviors and to think as a collective.

The spread of compulsory education for girls within a national education system established a foundation for women to improve their social status. Female students whose families could afford to send them to public women's higher school studied overtly gendered subjects like domestic science and "moral instruction," but they also could take classes in literature, history, geography, and science.[1] Collective experiences became available to young Japanese women and included sharing the same schedule, routines, and resources within an educational institution, where relationships could be formed through literary, artistic, and social activities. With advanced literacy, women could engage with print media as readers and writers. While these opportunities may have been restricted along gendered avenues of participation, they were markedly distinct from the networks available to women prior to the Meiji period.

When we consider girls' and women's education of the Meiji period, we often focus on the female students and the influence of the schoolgirl (*jogakusei*) on the Meiji cultural imagination. But there was also a greater need for educated women to instruct these girls. Women who received various degrees of training in the late Tokugawa and early Meiji periods experienced new social opportunities as teachers. Leading female educators at girls' schools were able to make curricular choices through defining specific occupations as suitable for women by shaping ideals and creating new opportunities.

Women who were educated in the early to mid-Meiji period in both traditional and modern subjects acquired that knowledge primarily through a rigorous classical Chinese education and used it as a foundation to disseminate knowledge to women as professional educators and writers.[2] Thus, to understand the foundational thinking of key members of the first cohort of educated Meiji women and those who became educators of women, we must examine the role that a classical Chinese education played in preparing them.

The concept of traditional education, associated with imperial rule and a native Japanese morality, included *kanbun* (classical Chinese) instruction, which played an important role in the early national curriculum. *Kanbun* took its place within the secondary school curriculum despite resistance from Western-minded officials, including former members of the Meirokusha (Meiji Six Society), the intellectual society founded by the educational statesman Mori Arinori (1847–89) to promote "civilization and enlightenment" through the propagation of Western ideas. Charter members included prominent educator Fukuzawa Yukichi (1835–1901), political thinker Katō Hiroyuki (1836–1916), and even Confucian humanists who were sympathetic to Westernization, such as Nishimura Shigeki (1828–1902) and Nakamura Masanao (1832–91). In the Meiji period, *kanbun* proficiency conveyed an "ethos of learnedness" that was not necessarily tied to a role as a government official but nonetheless held some authority in itself.[3] This was because knowledge of *kanbun* was a sign of status and ability not readily available to all and was a form of literacy coveted by ambitious men of the Meiji period. But this field of study was in transition and "was compelled . . . in the face of strident criticism and in the battle for survival to transform itself, to outfit itself for the changing times—in effect, to modernize itself."[4] Tensions arose between those who viewed Westernization as a source of national empowerment and the traditionalists who demanded that native Japanese culture—which included classical Chinese elements—be protected from incursion by Western ideas.

Many of the traditionalists in the Meiji government were Sinologists (*kangakusha*) and Confucian scholars (*jugakusha*) whose writings appear in Meiji-period textbooks and who joined the Meiji government as advisors. Many were also supporters of the *Kinnō tōbaku* (honor the emperor, destroy the *bakufu*), a movement of samurai who sought to oust the Tokugawa *bakufu* (or shogunate) to return power to the emperor. With the formation of the Meiji emperor's court, former pro-imperial scholars were hired as government officials. It was they who obstructed politicians' efforts to enforce a Westernized national culture by emphasizing Chinese studies in the early national curriculum.

In the midst of this conflict, the imperial court proved the strongest advocate for the traditionalists. The emperor received guidance on political issues from his appointed advisors, or *jihō*, such as his closest advisor and tutor, the Confucianist Motoda Nagazane (or Eifu, 1818–91), who spoke freely with him about their concerns on issues such as national security and diplomacy. Even after the *jihō* system was dismantled in 1879, Motoda in particular remained a trusted advisor of the emperor.[5] During Emperor Mutsuhito's tours of Japan from 1876 to 1881, Motoda took pains to demonstrate to the emperor the failure of English-centered curricula that were popular in a number of private primary schools. Bewildered primary school students would be brought before the emperor, who would ask them to explain how their English instruction was useful to them. They were unable to answer him.[6]

This exercise seemed to have the intended effect, as seen in the Imperial Will on Education (*Kyōgaku seishi*, 教学聖旨), authored by Motoda in 1879. This document described the emperor's disappointment in the state of primary education across Japan, as he had witnessed it himself, particularly given that early Meiji educational reforms had been implemented in his name.[7] The document called unequivocally for the Ministry of Education to make moral instruction based on a Confucian model its primary focus. Motoda thus sided with the Eastern-oriented traditionalists, who opposed the mid-Meiji government's Western-oriented progressives and their educational policies.[8]

The battle between imperial traditionalists and Western-minded policy makers was evident in various debates over Japanese cultural and intellectual identity, such as the question of adopting *kana* (syllabic writing system) or *rōmaji* (romanization of Japanese using roman, or Latin, script) as the written language of the modern Japanese people.[9] Traditionalists were already sensitive to the declining interest and the outright antagonism of pro-Westernizing officials in the government toward the continued use of classical Chinese as the language of politics, particularly when Itō Hirobumi (1841–1909) was prime minister and installed Mori Arinori, who was minister of education from 1885 to 1887.[10] Advocates for Westernization like Mori sought to remove *kanji* from the written language altogether, while proponents of scientific and Western subjects in primary and secondary schools targeted *kanbun* for permanent removal from curricula. For example, when the linguist Ueda Kazutoshi (1867–1937), the director of the Specialized Education Bureau (*Senmon gakumu kyoku*), led the Higher Council on Education (*Kōtō kyōiku kaigi*) between 1899 and 1903, he attempted to remove the subject of *kanbun* (*kanbun ka*) from the middle school curriculum. Furthermore, Ueda proposed to integrate *kanbun* studies into the subject of *kokugo ka* (Japanese studies), thereby deprioritizing it within the curriculum, which set off an outcry among Sinologists within and outside of Tokyo, leading to a petition that was submitted to the lower house of the Diet in 1901 to prevent the subject's removal.

There were other skirmishes over the role *kanbun* literacy would play on the cultural and political landscape. Despite the Japanese victory in the Sino-Japanese War of 1894–95, Sinologist Miura Kanō observes, Japan's military dominance over China contributed to a national interest in understanding the "real China" (*genjitsu no Shina*). This growing interest resulted in the implementation of "Chinese historical studies" (*Shina shigaku*) as a middle school subject, later to be replaced by "Oriental studies" (*tōyōgaku*).[11]

Imperial court officials also intervened in support of *kanbun* studies, and in 1902 the Imperial Educational Association (*Teikoku kyōikukai*, 1883–1944) established a research division to examine *kanbun* pedagogy (*kanbun kyōjuhō*). In 1903 they issued a ruling on the status of *kanbun* in the middle school curriculum, stating, "*Kanbun* and *kokugo* will be given equal status [but would be integrated under the subject title that would recognize *kanbun*'s importance] and will be called '*Kokugo* and *Kanbun*' [*kokugo oyobi kanbun ka*]."[12] These subjects were not meant to be exclusive to boys' schools and appear also to have been taught in girls' schools.[13]

Traditional education in the form of Confucian teachings that provided moral guidance may have appealed to the Eastern-oriented political advisors like Motoda Nagazane as suitable for women to teach female students to be docile, obedient, and industrious. Yet the application of such training yielded unanticipated modern benefits. Both traditional and modern government officials like Motoda and Itō agreed that women should be useful to government and that figures like the empress could be effective beyond the walls of the imperial quarters. Thus Japanese women were recruited by government officials in search of emissaries into the world of Western women, a world that was not available to the men of Japan but contained gendered secrets of civilized power that were essential to Japan's global status.

The New *Kōkyū* of Meiji Empress Haruko

Of the women to be discussed in this book, the most educated and politically powerful was Empress Haruko. Ichijō Masako (1849–1914)—known as Haruko during her tenure as empress of Japan (and as Empress Dowager Shōken after Emperor Meiji's death)—represented the height of Japanese women's privilege during the Meiji period. As the wife of the Meiji emperor, Mutsuhito (1852–1912), she was presented as the "mother" of the modern Japanese nation-state and as a powerful symbol of nationalism and imperial authority. Despite that a great deal of research on Haruko exists in Japanese, she has not been a central subject of analysis within English-language studies of Meiji women's history and literature.[14] Haruko was the third daughter of Ichijō Tadaka of the Fujiwara clan (1812–1863), a former *sadaijin* (minister of the left), and rose to the pinnacle of feminine privilege when she was crowned empress. Empress Haruko's activities are well recorded in her official chronicle, *Shōken kōtaigō jitsuroku* (Empress Dowager Shōken's official record), and in the *Meiji tennō ki* (Emperor Meiji's official records). She is known to have actively supported charitable efforts for the poor and for girls' education and advocated for change in the social opportunities available to women during her rule.[15] Yet we cannot attribute her advocacy entirely to her own individual motivations, for her activities were guided by government advisors: her charitable efforts were modeled after those of her Western counterparts, and official government reports relied upon the traditional Confucian view of a ruler's benevolence toward her subjects to explain her actions. What we can gather from court records and accounts of her court women was that she was a willing and enthusiastic participant. She left her mark on Meiji history by exercising her considerable intellect in the execution of her responsibilities.

Empress Haruko was groomed to be selected as a suitable consort for Mutsuhito and was chosen on the strength of her family lineage as well as her scholarly and artistic achievements. The notable events chronicled in the empress' *Official Record* prior to her ascension to the status of empress are limited to deaths, births, illness, marriages, honors, and academic and artistic achievements. Her early introduction to education reflected her elite pedigree. Donald Keene summarizes her talents as they were noted in the *Meiji tennō ki*:

> As a small child (between the ages of three and four) she had been able to read aloud the poetry in the anthology of *Kokinshū*, and at five she had composed *tanka* of her own. At seven she had done *sodoku* reading of a text in classical Chinese under the guidance of the Confucian scholar Nukina Masanori, with whom she also studied calligraphy. At twelve she had begun *koto* lessons and later also studied the *shō*, she was fond of *nō* and enjoyed singing passages from the plays as breaks from her studies. She had studied the tea ceremony and flower arrangement with masters of the day. She had never suffered any major illness, perhaps because she had been vaccinated against smallpox when she was eight.[16]

To this list, Empress Haruko's Offical Records add that at the age of seven she studied *Sanjikyō* (Three Character Classic) and *Rongo* (Analects). The eventual application of her knowledge to her role as empress sheds light on how "traditional" knowledge could be tapped to create new pedagogical practices and educational policies for women. In the empress, we see the influence of Confucianism cultivated in the Meiji Japanese context and the emergence of an imperialist and nationalist image of motherhood and public service.

In the Meiji imperial court, strict hierarchies and severe inequity shaped the lives of those women who served, strategized, collaborated, and competed with one another. Close examination of the most visible and admired Japanese women of the era, particularly those tied to the Meiji empress, provides insight into how certain permitted public activities, such as state dinners, diplomatic meetings, and inaugural events for educational institutions, were part of government efforts to establish Japan as a modern nation. Empress Haruko's activities during her reign provide a vibrant picture of how she and her immediate subjects managed and navigated the gendered conditions produced by the ideological shifts of the time.

Essential for Empress Haruko's power was the restructuring of the *kōkyū* (imperial residence), which was carried out from 1869 to 1873. The *kōkyū*, also referred to as the *dairi*, was a special sphere restricted to the emperor, the empress, and numerous court women of varying ranks and responsibilities. The imperial court had since at least the ninth century employed talented women of aristocratic lineage to engage in court rituals and cultural activities of unparalleled aesthetic excellence. Prior to the Meiji period, the *kōkyū*, which can be literally translated as "rear court" or "anterior court" and which literary scholar Joshua Mostow describes as the "imperial harem," had drawn its personnel exclusively from the aristocratic families of the *kuge* (pre-Meiji court nobility).[17] The level of the power and prestige of women at the imperial court is demonstrated in literary masterpieces of the Heian period (794–1185), such as the fiction and commentaries written by the court women Murasaki Shikibu (b. 978?) and Sei Shōnagon (966–1017?). Prior to the Meiji period, during the late Tokugawa period there was a resurgence of interest in the works of Heian court women, as nativist scholars argued for a national legacy of native culture and identity. In these works, the imperial residence was the subject and source of cultural capital even when the military-centered rule of the shogunate reduced it to virtual poverty. As anthropologist Takie Lebra points out, the legacy of the imperial court had become a source of cultural legitimacy for military rulers in the Tokugawa period (1603–1868), during which noble women married into *daimyō* (domainal lord) households: "The assimilation of court culture by the Tokugawa was inseparable from the shoguns' political practice of marrying women of the court."[18] Even so, apart from literary depictions of court life, the occupants of the imperial court were shrouded in mystery from most of the populace, including the aristocracy.

For new Meiji political leaders like Itō Hirobumi to be seen as legitimate leaders, it was necessary to also reshape the aristocratic system to include the new elites. This led to the formation in 1884 of a new aristocracy (*shin kazoku*). Former samurai who rose to powerful positions in the Meiji government were assigned new ranks created with the issuance of the *kazokurei*, an imperial ordinance that established the basic structure of the nobility and was in effect until 1945.[19] Concurrent to this shuffling of statuses, which allowed former samurai to become titled barons, was an effort to incorporate the victors of the Meiji Restoration as comparable in importance to the old aristocracy.

The imperial court itself harbored aristocratic influences that the Meiji oligarchs were eager to dismantle. Hidden from view for centuries, the imperial court women had served under a strictly hierarchical order of administration, which was restructured and invigorated during the Meiji period. In the early Meiji period, the most experienced and ambitious of these court women—whose predecessors had guarded imperial customs even during the centuries of relative impoverishment and neglect under shogunal rule—were ready to enforce the traditions and rituals of past emperors in the Meiji era. Itō Hirobumi and fellow members of the Meiji oligarchy sought to loosen the grip of the court women, who had held power under previous imperial reigns and who would likely resist the modernization deemed necessary to elevate Japan's international standing. In the guise of reforms (*kaikaku*), the old *kōkyū* was dismantled in a single day on August 1, 1871, as the highest-ranking court women of the *kōkyū* were dismissed en masse from their positions. The empress was then given authority in the court and direct access to the emperor as his ruling partner.[20] Without the removal of these guardians of ancient customs, it would have been impossible to modernize the Meiji imperial court: they would have staunchly objected to any Westernization of the imperial dress and lifestyle that the new government officials saw as essential to raising Japan's international image as a "civilized" nation.

The *kōkyū* reforms also led to the inclusion of more nonhereditary *kuge*, allowing new *jokan* (court women) to be recruited not only from the aristocracy but also from lesser ranks. Divisions remained between hereditary *kuge* and recruits from more recently promoted families of the new aristocracy, who were considered by the old guard to have an inauthentic claim to aristocratic rank. Even as the pool of titled families expanded, divisions were maintained, for example, within the careful distribution of tasks between those who were permitted to enter the most private rooms of the emperor and empress (limited to those of old lineage) and those who worked only beyond those walls (those of newer aristocratic lineage).[21]

Former *jokan* Yamakawa Michiko published a memoir in 1960 of her time serving the emperor and empress in the last few years of Meiji's rule. Her memoir has since served as a valuable resource for information about the *kōkyū*, which was accessible to so few. Yamakawa was of *kuge* lineage, which was important because this pre-Restoration aristocracy descended from nobles who had been permitted entry into the emperor's private quarters (*seiryōden*) in the imperial palace.[22] Yamakawa's family status raised her above other more experienced attendants in the *kōkyū* and from early on allowed her to serve in close proximity to the imperial couple. She depicts in detail the division of space and labor in which some *jokan* were designated to carry food or clothing only as far as the hallway surrounding the innermost quarters, whereupon the delivered items would be handed to those attendants assigned to serve the couple directly.[23]

The Meiji period marks the first time that nonaristocratic women served as imperial ladies-in-waiting on the basis of their talents. The ideal of feminine excellence that they represented also changed in the Meiji period. Rather than representing aristocratic lineage, commoner women could offer intellect and knowledge as the main justification for their service. In this light, we can better understand where the two other women discussed in this book fit in. Nakajima Shōen (or Kishida Toshiko), the daughter of a merchant family, was employed as a *goyō gakari* (court attendant). Shimoda Utako, the daughter of a minor samurai family, held a position much higher than Shōen's, for Utako rose through the ranks with unprecedented speed. Nevertheless, even Utako experienced the humiliation of being a *jokan* of lesser rank, as discussed by writer and activist Yamakawa Kikue in a widely cited anecdote in which Utako's father had complained to Yamakawa Kikue's mother of the terrible treatment Utako received in court and insisted that it was not a suitable place for a country samurai's daughter.[24] Here we have some inkling of the complexity of the identity formation of imperial court women: they were obliged to observe the rules, both ancient and new, of the *kōkyū*, while also projecting an image of refinement, eliteness, and education.

Haruko was incorporated into the nation-state in ways unique to her gender and status. First, as partner to the emperor, she embodied one-half of Japan's civilized monarchy. Elevating the empress' status so that it was more like the status of Western queens improved Japan's image. As such, she was presented also as a "mother" of the modern Japanese nation-state, serving an important new role within the "family" state. Haruko's public activities included court rituals as well as public ceremonies that emphasized her gendered role. She supported charitable efforts for the poor and for girls' education; at the same time, she was the fashionable icon of a newly encouraged public visibility for elite women. Artistic representations, such as colorful woodblock prints, of the empress and her court women were in popular demand, feeding the public's fascination with this new kind of celebrity and luxury. She also demonstrated a charisma that historian Katano Masako describes as a "shaman-like persona," which helped her to embody "the future of modern Japan."[25]

The empress' public presence gave her unprecedented authority. The empress' attitude toward the acquisition of knowledge, her embrace of her gendered diplomatic role as host to Western dignitaries and their wives, and her serene demeanor were a calming force in the new *kōkyū*. While government ministers, particularly Itō Hirobumi, sought to Westernize women's style of dress, it was Haruko who successfully made that shift, authoring a memorandum (*oboshimeshi*) on the subject in 1886.[26] With this document, she spearheaded the shift to Western dress for the women of the imperial court and the aristocracy. When she paid her first visit to the Peeresses' School (Kazoku Jogakkō)—the school designated for daughters of the Japanese aristocracy—she appeared in Western clothing. She identified potential informants of Western cultural practices, consulting with the Prussian courtier Ottmar von Mohl (1846–1922) and his wife Wanda von Mohl (née Countess von der Groeben) to learn about the customs of European courts. Having served in the court of Empress Augusta and Emperor Wilhelm in Berlin, Ottmar von Mohl was appointed to advise the Meiji court on etiquette and court customs along the lines of European royal practices.[27]

But even as Empress Haruko stepped into a new, Occidentalizing role, she remained conscious of domestic demands that privileged a uniquely Japanese identity. She believed in the imperial system and the deity of the emperor and had the discipline and foresight to adapt to the demands of the era. Haruko was also guided by Itō and court advisor Motoda Nagazane, who conveyed to her the necessity of improving women's status and education to enhance Japan's image as an enlightened nation. Confucian traditionalists such as Motoda fared particularly well in their attempts to mold the moral guidelines that would be promoted and exemplified by the emperor and empress.[28] Despite sharing opposing views with Motoda on the question of Westernization, Itō trusted him to assist with the reform of the imperial court. This was advantageous for Itō, whom Emperor Mutsuhito disliked and whose suggestion to Westernize the court he resisted.[29] It was Motoda and Empress Haruko who persuaded Mutsuhito to make the social policy changes that they understood to be in the best interest of the imperial system.

Empress Haruko seemed to adapt to the demands of modern monarchical rule more effectively than Mutsuhito. The empress stepped in to carry out tasks that the emperor refused, or was unable, to fulfill. Her duties included showing imperial support for new industries, including gold, coal, and silver mining, which had begun under Tokugawa rule. On October 25,

1884, for example, she visited the Shinagawa glassworks upon its sale by the Meiji government to two investors, Count Inaba Masakuni and Nishimura Katsuzō. She also helped to cultivate the image of a healthy relationship between the court and the Meiji cabinet by having tea at Itō's manor following her visit to the factory.[30]

Royal Motherhood for the Meiji Period

One of the great contradictions of Empress Haruko's role in the Meiji imperial court was the fact that in the era of *ryōsai kenbo*, which so praised the work of the devoted wife and wise mother, she did not give birth to an heir. There was a clear divide between her and the emperor's concubines (*tenji* and *gotenji*), who were given court titles but were relegated to lesser roles. The empress' increased power was directly related to a new kind of intimacy with the emperor, as the two were presented officially as a monogamous couple in the manner of their contemporary Western monarchies. Due to the empress' inability to bear children, and ostensibly against the Meiji emperor's own wishes, as Donald Keene explains, the emperor was served by at least six other court women as nocturnal companions and potential mothers to imperial heirs: "Even if the emperor had been reluctant to share his bed with another woman, he had the duty of providing an heir to the throne; and from about this time [1873], he spent his nights with carefully selected women of the high nobility in the hopes that one or more of them would conceive."[31] While advisors like the chief chamberlain, Tokudaiji Sanetsune, asked the emperor "to summon more court ladies to his side" out of worry for the scarcity of male heirs and "as an act of piety toward his ancestors," Keene points out that the emperor did not take his advice.[32] As Keene surmises, "the strict manner in which his heir, the future emperor Taishō, was raised suggests that Meiji had come to disapprove of the profligacy that had been a traditional privilege of the sovereign."[33] It is important to note that such a return to past practices took place even as the empress held unprecedented authority within and beyond the court.[34] Therefore, it was possible that, in the era of *ryōsai kenbo*, the role of the "good mother" could be carried out whether or not one had given birth.

The implications of Haruko's "good mother" role were complex. One high-ranking court woman, Takakura Toshiko, is quoted in Yamakawa Kikue's *Onna nidai no ki* (A record of two generations of women) describing the empress as the personification of the ethical manual for women attributed to Kaibara Ekiken (1630–1714), *Onna daigaku* (Greater learning for women). Takakura comments on the symbolic role of the empress as an ideal monarch, whose body was marked by neither childbirth nor even sexual relations. This mark of a kind of moral "purity" on Haruko's part emerges still as a kind of failure, as Takakura is quoted saying that the empress "was pitied even by the pregnant *jokan*."[35] Katano Masako asserts, however, that amid fierce competition for the emperor's affection among potential mothers of heirs to the imperial throne, the empress was able to remain above the fray, safe from fear of rejection or demotion. Katano states further, "not bearing children allowed the empress to maintain a distance from the *jokan*, and appears to have allowed her to take a rational approach to life" (*riseitekina seikatsu taido*).[36] The division of labor that Katano asserts between the empress and the women of the emperor's harem shows the latter to be reduced to their bodies. Removed from the duty to give birth afforded Haruko privileges reserved for male aristocrats of the Meiji imperial bureaucracy.

Some court women had observed also that Empress Haruko exhibited "a confidence that allowed her to be deeply compassionate and playful toward the *jokan*—she never failed to be vigilant of her own position within that period, using her knowledge to play the role of moderator even as she appeared to be doing nothing of the sort."[37] The empress' behavior as witnessed by her subjects gave no indication of bitterness toward the emperor's concubines and in fact appears to have been characterized by warmth and affection, particularly toward Yanagiwara Naruko (1859–1943), the Taishō emperor's birth mother.[38] This may suggest the empress' resilience under social scrutiny, but it may also indicate that the source of her identity as empress was not tied to childbirth, although elements of it were borrowed from the idealized image of the royal mother.

Of the Western monarchs who served as models for the Meiji empress, Queen Victoria of England (1819–1901) and Duchess Louise of Mecklenburg-Strelitz (1776–1810) were two of the most influential. Both women bore at least nine children, including future heirs, and as a result were able to achieve the status of a kind of "sacred mother" of the Christian tradition.[39] The level of respect and authority Victoria and Louise enjoyed could not have been achieved by Haruko because, as art historian Wakakuwa Midori argues, "not only was the Japanese Empress not prolific [with regards to childbearing], but she was also chained by the shackles of the Confucian tradition, making her failures all the more apparent."[40] Wakakuwa asserts further that the Meiji empress embodied the subordination of Japanese women, and of housewives, who were essential to the construction of a national order primarily through the "noble" deed of nurturing their families and future citizens.[41] As such, Haruko's infertility was widely remarked upon and her virtue was seen as residing in her devotion to Mutsuhito's heir as though she were his biological mother. Wakakuwa is right in stating that Haruko was subordinate to Mutsuhito. But even in her subordination, she held some form of privilege that reveals her sway over others' lives.

Meiji Kanbun *and Moral Textbooks for Women*

The Meiji women who were educated in *kanbun* studies participated in the era's new economy by publishing textbooks and commentaries and working as instructors. *Kanbun* textbooks and their variants were compilations of annotated excerpts from classical Chinese texts, as well as translations of Chinese texts into Japanese. This genre of textbook was available throughout the Tokugawa period. Compilations often included works by classical Chinese authors like Mencius (372–289 BCE, known in Japanese as Mōshi) and Liu Xiang (77–6 BCE, known in Japanese as Ryū Kyō), as well as Japanese-authored Chinese texts deemed especially important for girls, such as "*Kenpu nanigashi den*" (Tale of an upright woman) from the Sinologist and physician Gamō Shigeaki's (1833–1901) *Kinsei ijin den* (Biographies of recent great personages). Such texts, including many written or annotated during the Tokugawa period, were published in *kanbun* collections during the Meiji period. While the republication of Tokugawa-era texts might appear to reflect a continuation of premodern learning, their circulation in the Meiji period, both as *kanbun* study manuals and as moral guides, constitutes a historically specific manifestation of Chinese classics and Confucian ideals being geared toward modern Japanese girls and women.

A handful of *kanbun* textbooks for women were published in the 1890s and early 1900s. *Joshi kanbun tokuhon dai 4-hen* (Women's *kanbun* reader 4), for instance, was edited and compiled by Utsunomiya Takako (?–?) and revised by the educator Miwada Masako (1843–1923).[42] Its prose is in *kanbun kundokutai* (classical Chinese word order with diacritic marks to indicate Japanese reading order), and it includes excerpts from essays by both Chinese and Japanese authors of *kanbun*. The more recent excerpts were not meant exclusively for female readers, but depict model individuals, both male and female, who had led virtuous lives, such as "*Yamaguchi Shig-*

enobu den" by Gamō Shigeaki and "*Ōishi Chikara*" by the Mito School Confucianist Aoyama Nobumitsu (1807–71).

Various classical Chinese readers (*kanbun tokuhon*)—such as the *Joshi kanbun tokuhon dai 4-hen* and the *Chūgaku kanbun tokuhon* (Middle school *kanbun* reader) published in 1894—share several common essays, mostly by Japanese authors, so there was not a strict differentiation between texts that were suitable only for boys and those also suitable for girls.[43] One particularly provocative essay from *Joshi kanbun tokuhon dai 4-hen* that addresses female *kanbun* students is Nakamura Ritsuen's (1806–81) "*Joshi o shite sho o yomashimu bekarazaru ron*" (Women should not read).[44] In his essay, Ritsuen argues against teaching girls to read because they will become arrogant, promiscuous, or unmarriageable. He even suggests that education would strip them of their femininity, without which they would become "monsters" (*yōbutsu*). Ritsuen admits that on occasion a woman might have the potential to become a great scholar like Bān Zhāo (45–ca. 116), China's foremost female scholar and the author of *Precepts for Women* (*Nüjie*), or a great writer like Murasaki Shikibu, the author of *The Tale of Genji* (*Genji monogatari*). He even suggests that women could learn the female virtues, respect their elders, and follow the ways of heaven through reading but insists that such instances were rare.[45] Ritsuen concludes by calling on men to cease teaching their daughters to read. As within Ritsuen's own collected works, the essay was followed by commentaries from individuals who alternately agreed and disagreed with Ritsuen's argument. These responses were not included in the girls' *kanbun* textbooks, however. Given the high level of *kanbun* literacy of the textbook's editor, Miwada Masako, the inclusion of the essay might have served as a warning to women to be aware of the risks of learning too much or of the likelihood that reading might even "ruin" them.[46] It is also possible, however, that the essay was meant to serve as a warning to students that such objections to their education existed among *kanbun* scholars and that they should either be careful of how they revealed their proficiency or be prepared for censure. Their exposure to this essay exemplifies the conundrum of educated women and the process of educating them during the Meiji period.

The traditional nature of the *kanbun* style did not dictate the textbooks' content, however, as *kanbun* textbooks of the 1890s designated for female students did not always adhere to what might be considered traditional topics. The 1901 *Joshi kokubun tokuhon* (Women's national literature reader), edited by Kokubu Misako and published by Aoyama Seikichi, for instance, includes scientific content. It includes an essay on breastfeeding excerpted from *Fuei shinsetsu* (1859), the *kanbun* translation of Benjamin Hobson's *Treatise on Midwifery and Diseases of Children*, as well as an excerpt of William Alexander Parsons Martin's (1827–1916) *Kakubutsu nyūmon* (Introduction to underlying principles), a textbook of elemental physics written in *kanbun*.[47]

In the same way that *kanbun* stood in as "tradition" for the scholars advising Emperor Meiji, moral teachings attributed to classical Chinese texts—but no longer limited to that style of writing—also represented Japanese tradition. In keeping with the sentiments expressed in the Imperial Will on Education, discussed earlier, the Meiji empress also contributed to women's educational materials through patronage. Two guides to morality (*dōtokusho*) were compiled and published by order of the empress through the Imperial Ministry: *Meiji kōsetsuroku* (Meiji record of filial tales) and *Fujo kagami* (A model for women).[48] While these texts are not works of *kanbun*, their focus on morality is similar to many instructional guides that were translated or adapted from classical Chinese works into Japanese. *Meiji kōsetsuroku*, published in 1877, was compiled by Kondō Yoshiki (1801–80), a *kokugaku* (national learning) scholar and poet who served as one of the imperial court's literary advisors. It is a collection of stories about Japanese men and women who demonstrate great virtue in dire circumstances. Many of the women depicted in the collection are driven to protect themselves against the threat of violence, including rape. Historian Katano Masako argues that the boldness and even ferocity characterizing these heroically virtuous women suggest Empress Haruko's progressive view of women's more active role as the guardian of the family and home.[49] Art historian Wakakuwa Midori, however, argues that the stories' emphasis on women's chastity—which these characters defend even to the point of sacrificing their lives—is fundamentally patriarchal and contradicts any progressive interpretation of the violence that women endure in these tales to prove their worth.[50] Wakakuwa's point is crucial. Yet a division remains between the empress, who held the authority to disperse narratives that she selected and exemplified, and the narratives that were meant to educate her readers. Empress Haruko consciously enforced a narrative at the apex upon which she stood, and her reinforcement of that privilege and of the subjugation and objectification of other women is not a rare occurrence in modern women's history.

The second imperially requisitioned moral guide appeared a decade later, in 1887. *Fujo kagami*, compiled by Nishimura Shigeki, is unlike *Meiji kōsetsuroku* in that the majority of the women it depicts are Western or Chinese. The prefatory material includes an editor's preface composed in *kanbun*, a publishing convention of the late Tokugawa and early Meiji periods—indicating that Nishimura anticipated an audience that was familiar with this convention. Many of the women featured in the tales were the wives of great Western men, and the women's actions were more or less interchangeable with those of the chaste women described in classic Confucian moral tales. Four types of feminine conduct are covered in the collection, corresponding to the Confucian notion of the Four Virtues: women's morality, women's speech, women's comportment, and women's work. In addition to the guide's references to Western as well as Chinese women, what made it distinctly modern were the tasks carried out by the women, which included bookkeeping, domestic management, and the education of children, both male and female. Thus the textbook fulfilled a utilitarian function by offering models for young Meiji women to follow. The aim was to argue that traditional morality would be compatible with and improve upon modern practices.

Elite women were the primary targets of *Fujo kagami*. Upon its publication, it was distributed as a gift from the empress to all the students at the Peeresses' School to help prepare them to be the wives of Japan's future great men: its politicians, scientists, and military officers.[51] Women were being called upon to adapt to the specific needs of their respective husbands' careers, which might require more education than had been previously expected of Japanese women. The virtuous Western women depicted in *Fujo kagami*, in addition to being competent wives, also introduced Japan's upper-class women to the practice of charity work for the orphaned, indigent, and injured, a new kind of permissible activity beyond the home.

As part of the imperial initiative to incorporate traditional Chinese studies into Japanese studies, these morality textbooks were rooted in Confucian moral guides and anthologies, but they offered a new, modern lineup of role models. These works, and particularly the later *Fujo kagami*, were part of an effort to create a national ethic—one that specifically called on women to contribute by fulfilling their gender-specific roles within and beyond the home. Wakakuwa is critical of *Fujo kagami* as a work that presents Confucianism "clothed in Western gowns with bustles."[52] But we might borrow from Koyama Shizuko's analysis of *ryōsai kenbo* and identify Meiji nation-building efforts as the reverse: modern concepts in traditional or

Confucian garb that was distinct from Edo-period Confucian schools of thought.[53] The Confucian ideals of virtuous wives and mothers, particularly as represented in *Fujo kagami*, are indeed compatible with the idealized image of the bourgeois middle-class housewife in late nineteenth-century England and United States and are themselves modern and cannot be easily detangled from that image.[54]

Moral education for women relied on a Confucian legacy but was drawn from multiple competing schools of Confucian thought. Koyama has suggested that the moral (*dōtoku*) instruction for women that emerged in Confucian studies during this period was the source of *ryōsai kenbo*, the ideological core of Meiji women's education. She states that "we cannot adequately understand *ryōsai kenbo* thought without considering its differences from the Edo view of women and the relation of women to the modern nation-state" and goes so far as to say that *ryōsai kenbo* "is not necessarily directly linked to Confucianism" because the expression dates only to the Meiji period and analogous terms in Korean and Chinese did not appear until the late nineteenth and early twentieth centuries, and then only as imported concepts from Japan.[55] The Confucian ideals that underlay the aggressive promotion of *ryōsai kenbo* ideology succeeded in shaping women's modern roles and constructing a gendered nationalism in the Meiji period. As Koyama has argued, *ryōsai kenbo* is a "*modern* way of thinking related to, and having much in common with, views of a woman's desirable qualities in the context of postwar Japanese society as well as in modern Western nations and beyond."[56] Thus the image of a domesticated Meiji woman embodying the tenets of *ryōsai kenbo* appears to have more in common with later generations of Japanese women than with those who were proficient in *kanbun*, who served as administrators, educators, authors, and promoters of women's learning in the Meiji period.

Traditional Training for Modern Employment

Literary scholars Atsuko Sakaki and Mari Nagase have examined women's *kanbun* proficiency and the social acceptance of their composition of *kanshi* (classical Chinese poetry) in the late Tokugawa period. In the introduction, I discussed how *kanbun* proficiency in the early Meiji period was gendered male and considered indispensible for male politicians in particular.[57] As women were excluded from most government posts in the Meiji period, *kanbun* was most useful to women employed outside the home, especially in educational, diplomatic, or charitable work. While there are well-known examples of male commentators decrying the use of *kanbun* phrases by Meiji schoolgirls, as I will discuss in more detail in chapter 2, those women with proficiency in the Meiji period appear to have benefited from the so-cial esteem that *kanbun* literacy inspired in educated and elite circles.[58] The particular uses of their skills indicate that *kanbun* proficiency was a source of social capital by which women were able to garner legitimacy in the press and authority in their professional lives as educators and writers.

Kanbun-educated women were somewhat rare but not extinct. Printing technology and the growth of literacy meant that once they were given prominent roles as educators and writers, these women were visible and capable of contributing to Meiji discourse. Meiji women who were trained well in classical Chinese also tended to be familiar with major Confucian texts. Margaret Mehl, a historian of Meiji *kangaku juku* (private academies of Chinese learning), has written that *kanbun*'s "importance gradually de-clined from the late 1870s onwards" but also explains that "Chinese learning had represented the mainstream of scholarship and education before 1868 and remained important until the 1890s."[59]

Not only was the empress adept at *kanbun* scholarship, but she also had women in her court who joined her in her pursuit of further study. One such figure with close ties to the Meiji empress was Wakae Nioko (Shūran, 1835–81), who authored *Wage onna shishō* published posthumously in 1883, and was an annotated version of the *Onna shisho* (Four books for women), which had been translated first into Japanese in 1656.[60] Four books for women annotated in Japanese,. Nioko was a female Sinologist who carried over her extensive *kanbun* training from the late Tokugawa period into the mid-Meiji period. She was Empress Haruko's tutor before Haruko became an empress. Historian Sekiguchi Sumiko writes that Nioko exerted a great deal of influence over Haruko and inspired the empress' enthusiasm for the moral lessons in *Onna shisho*, which she set out to popularize with the an-notated edition as "the basic text for girls' education in modern Japan."[61] Nioko was given the moniker *kenpaku onna* (the petition woman) for the many petitions she submitted to the government that reflected her support of the *sonnō jōi* (revere the emperor, expel the barbarians) movement.[62]

Nioko makes an appearance in Meiji novelist and physician Mori Ōgai's (1862–1922) work of historical fiction "Tsuge Shirōzaemon" (1915).[63] Ōgai describes how in the wake of Tsuge Shirōzaemon's assassination of Yokoi

Heihachirō, who opened up Japan to Western medicine and technology, Nioko defends Tsuge's act by stating that "righteous subjects are a nation's strength and vigor" and insists that Yokoi deserved to die because he and his associates were guilty of "scheming to spread the Roman Church throughout all of Japan."[64]

The story is told from the perspective of Tsuge's son and through the letters he receives responding to his inquiries about his late father's life. Descriptions of Nioko are included at the end of the narrative as an addendum to Tsuge's life and controversial act. In the addendum, Nioko appears as an eccentric woman whose intellect and enthusiasm were evident to all who met her. Tateo, the uncle of the narrator's acquaintance Shiba Katsushige, recalls having met Nioko when he was a child: "The older [daughter] was an unusual woman: dark-complexioned, with no makeup whatever, her hair bound artlessly. I recall how, more than a match for any man, she heatedly engaged my father in argument. Even he said he could not stand up to such a woman. This was Nihoko [Nioko], probably."[65]

The descriptions of Nihoko are unflattering but do not dismiss her intellect:

> Nihoko was not a good-looking woman, but she was a talented one. When the Empress Shōken was still residing in her Ichijō home, Nihoko gave her lectures on Chinese works. Mimaki himself had attended Nihoko's lectures. Because she spoke out about matters of state, she was told to quit her position and was placed with a [member of the] Tanaka [family] employed by the Fushimi-no-miya family. Later because of an indiscretion, she was shunned by self-respecting folk; she then dwelt in isolated retirement in the vicinity of Akashi, in Suma, where it seems she died. Nihoko's poems have made their way here and there into the world.[66]

Ōgai's narrator quotes from the annals of Toda Tadayoshi to give further evidence of Nioko's role in the imperial court:

> Nihoko's advice seemed to play a considerable part in the selection of the Crown Princess who was destined to become Empress Shōken. In the sixth month of 1867, announcement was made of Empress Shōken's entrance into court, and shortly afterward women were chosen to serve as her upper and middle ladies-in-waiting; at this time Nihoko was again requested to come to the palace and give lessons.[67]

Toda Tadayoshi's account indicates that Nioko served as a de facto intermediary between Haruko and court officials seeking a suitable wife for the emperor. As the daughter of Wakae Shuridaibu (1812–72), who held a court rank and was a trusted colleague of the court noble Toda, Nioko also regularly visited the Ichijō home to tutor Haruko. She was, therefore, in a unique position to advocate for Haruko and vouch for Haruko's suitability as empress.[68] It is evident also that Nioko's knowledge of *kanbun* was sought out to ensure that Haruko was receiving the highest caliber of instruction even after becoming empress.

Female educators who rose to prominence in the Meiji period were regularly described as "fine ladies of the women's society" (*fujinkai no kifujin*), who included the wives of Meiji officials and members of the old aristocracy. In addition to Shimoda Utako, there were Hatoyama Haruko (1863–1938) and Yajima Kajiko (1833–1925).[69] Historian Margaret Mehl explains that Miwada Masako and Atomi Kakei (1840–1926) "did not fight for women's rights in opposition to the state and were not led by Western ideas," but they "helped redefine the role of women and shape a society with increasing educational opportunities for women."[70] Kakei's artistic talents as a painter and poet were well known, and she was invited to poetry gatherings (*o utakai*) in 1872 and 1879 that were attended by the empress. She also contributed to national exhibitions, such as the Oriental Art Fair (Tōyō Kaiga Kyōshinkai) of 1886, which exhibited works by fifteen *joryū gaka* (female painters).[71] Her father ran a *kangaku juku* to support his family in rural Osaka, and Kakei was educated in both the Japanese and Chinese classics. Through her father's employment with an aristocratic family in Kyoto, Kakei would later start a *juku* of her own, but she began teaching *kangaku* and painting to court ladies, and her reputation as an instructor for elite women grew. Kakei's *juku*, which eventually became Atomi Jogakkō (Atomi Girls' School), instructed girls in various subjects, including the Chinese classics. As Mehl explains, Kakei "aimed to provide her pupils with an education that would prepare them for their role as good wife and wise mother. Therefore, importance was attached to teaching practical subjects and arts as well as the Chinese and Japanese classics."[72] Thus, while the importance of *kanbun* as a subject of study was on the decline in the Meiji period in comparison to the late Tokugawa era, the existing literacy in *kanbun* among eligible bachelors made it advantageous to offer it as a subject to their prospective wives.

Shimoda Utako, whose career is discussed in detail in chapter 3, was a member of Empress Haruko's court whose *kanbun* proficiency was also crucial to her work as an educator and advocate for women's education. Utako hailed from a samurai family of Chinese studies scholars with non-conformist, anti-Tokugawa, pro-imperial political proclivities. Her maternal grandfather, Tōjō Kindai (or Nobuyasu, 1795–1878), was a well-known scholar of Chinese studies (*kangakusha*), and her father, Hirao Jūzō, was a Confucian scholar.[73] Both Sinologists supported the *kinnō* (revere the emperor) movement during the late Tokugawa period prior to the Meiji Restoration of 1868.[74] Jūzō was periodically arrested for criticism of the Tokugawa shogunate (or *bakufu*, twelfth to nineteenth centuries), and Utako was accustomed to his absence during her childhood. Having advocated for the restoration of imperial rule, both Kindai and Jūzō achieved some recognition in the early years of the Meiji era as state propagandists (*senkyōshi*) for the new government. But in keeping with their open criticism of the government and their support for a more prominent role for the emperor, they did not remain long in their new posts.[75] Tōjō Kindai also wrote an 1873 *kanbun* textbook for women entitled *Shōgaku hitsudoku onna sanjikyō* (Essential reading Three Character Classic for women), which provided his commentary on the *Three Character Classic* (*Sanjikyō*). As a descendent of Sinologists, Utako—like a number of her fellow female Meiji educators—studied classical Chinese in addition to more traditional feminine curricula of *waka* (traditional Japanese poetry) and Confucian manuals for girls. Utako managed her *kanbun* proficiency with discretion. Her biographer notes that, as soon as Utako entered court service in 1872, she ceased composing *kanshi* and writing in *kanbun*. This may have been due to the fact that she was highly valued for her *waka* composition, a skill that was considered more traditionally feminine. But years later, when Utako traveled to England in 1893 and resided there for almost two years to gather information on girls' education, she translated school regulations and wrote reports to be reviewed by court and government officials in *kanbun*.[76]

Empress Haruko's court provided a network of education and employment for women of talent as well as lineage. Many of these women had few options for occupations apart from teaching, or marriage. The imperial court offered public positions that went beyond the confines of family or community, which former *jokan* Yamakawa Michiko states was her reason for agreeing to serve.[77] With women of the aristocratic and commoner classes mixing as members of the imperial court, both traditional and modern forms of intellectual activity flourished beyond their court service.

Itō Hirobumi encouraged Haruko's interest and participation in government efforts to educate women, but it was an endeavor she carried out without prompting. She provided considerable monetary support for women's schools. To celebrate the inauguration of the Peeresses' School, the empress bequeathed one of her poems, which was set to music and served as the school song.[78] At a time when the necessity of educating girls was still being debated, the empress' support and patronage provided imperial legitimacy to the school's mission. Her charitable and educational activities—such as funding schools, tending wounded soldiers, and helping to establish the Red Cross in Japan—might have been informed by Confucianism, but it was her elite education in the late Tokugawa period that, at least in part, gave her the ability to adapt to extreme shifts in cultural and social expectations.

Conclusion

The empress commissioned two Meiji guidebooks for women, *Meiji kōsetsuroku* and *Fujo kagami*, both of which promoted Confucian tenets. To unpack how promoting Confucianism provided Haruko with the authority to serve as a female icon, it is necessary to examine how the combative relationship between women and Confucianism has been tackled in the previous literature. In her analysis of the complex gender and power networks at play for seventeenth-century female writers, Dorothy Ko does not see Confucianism as an entirely restrictive ideology for women:

> By implicating women as actors maneuvering to further their perceived interests from within the system, I see them as architects of concrete gender relations, the building blocks from which the overarching gender system was constructed. Instead of outright resistance or silencing, I describe processes of contestation and negotiation, whose meaning is ambivalent not only to us in hindsight but also to men and women at the time.[79]

But it is important to acknowledge that women have been subjugated in the name of Confucian principles. Wakakuwa Midori asserts that Confucianism, in addition to being a key component of the modern nation Japan became, was largely responsible for the severity of Japanese women's oppression:

The oppression of Japanese women was the most severe of the advanced nations. This was because Japan did not yet possess a civil morality, but still preserved the various systems of the premodern era, including misogyny, and assigned new national obligations to women. This was something akin to women dancing in their Western ball gowns, still shackled to the chains of Confucianism.[80]

Even if the empress' activities were Western in appearance and Confucian in their content, her position as subordinate and subject to the emperor and to the nation-state did not negate her authority. Haruko was the most visible and influential figure to actively promote a specific curriculum and vision for modern Japanese women; she enthusiastically served as an architect and spokesperson of this vision, promoting her own support for girls' education. She was not merely a puppet or a passive recipient of fixed tasks but an active negotiator reacting to the demands of the era. Her position as a modern monarch was defined neither by silence nor by resistance. She relied on Confucianism as "a cluster of ethical ideals" rather than as a monolithic ideology to justify her more public role.[81] Modernization of women's education in the Meiji era is as much a part of the concept of ryōsai kenbo in the formation of the modern woman as the invention of its Confucian origin, as Koyama suggests. Empress Haruko's power over her court and nation was informed by both Confucian ideals and modern practices that provided some of the language to articulate modern Japanese womanhood.

The concept of gendered power recognizes the multiplicity of networks that differ in their practices and import according to status and education. The employment opportunities that arose in the fields of education, textiles, and healthcare as a result of the empress' advocacy shaped the conditions under which women immediately around her and under her rule worked.

Meiji kanbun-educated women, especially those with ties to the imperial court, have been largely excluded from feminist histories of Japan. The examples of professional and public leadership they offer can help us to understand the emergence of women as a new social category, as constituents in Meiji society. Empress Haruko and the educated women who served in her court or were supported by her promoted a unique role for women in the nation-building project. Affiliation with the empress allowed some women to harness national educational systems to further their own personal and social ambitions. While officials, the media, and women themselves monitored women's groups, within those groups women held authority.

Leading educators of women in the mid- to late Meiji period received a traditional education, namely, instruction in classical Chinese and Japanese subjects. It was upon this foundation that they produced new models of national womanhood. Takashi Fujitani suggests that "the subject-citizen produced by the Japanese emperor-centered regime" was in fact not so different from "the hero of modern bourgeois society."[82] Likewise, the Meiji empress, who modeled a new kind of feminine achievement, exemplified characteristics of the bourgeois housewife then being introduced to Japan. This is meaningful, for as Wakakuwa Midori argues, the empress was essential to the formation of Japanese modernity as "the ideal model of women's nationalization (*kokuminka*), and as its living exemplar (*ikita mohan*)."[83] The empress' reputation as an avatar of ideal Meiji womanhood may have been reinforced by her patronage of some of Japan's most educated women, who went on to participate prominently in education and literary discourse during the Meiji era. The conditions of her reign clearly combine the conventions of the late Tokugawa period with new demands as understood and strategized by Meiji government officials.

Kanbun-educated women would not have been valued by the government without the imperial court's support nor without the court advisor's bias toward traditional education. This is seen in the educational texts that were produced by the government.

Empress Haruko and the women she appointed or supported as educators, especially those trained in traditional subjects, demonstrate greater feminine authority and a focusing of women's permissible public activities. Many *kanbun*-proficient women arrived at their proficiency through Confucian studies and found purpose in applying their knowledge to furthering education for women. That this did not lead directly to women's suffrage and equality does not erase the fact that women's labor and responsibility were at work within the institutions of Meiji power. Rather, understanding and accepting that such differences are part of modern social systems opened them to strategize ways to reshape and redistribute that power.

CHAPTER 2

FROM KISHIDA TOSHIKO
TO NAKAJIMA SHŌEN

A Meiji Classical Chinese Foundation
for a Modern Japanese Woman

Introduction

On April 7, 1882, a letter to the editor titled "Women Are Not As They
Should Be" appeared in the *Yomiuri shimbun* (Yomiuri newspaper). In it the
author, Katō Shihō (Hyōko) (1856–1923), a publisher of the newspaper,
complains about a recent troubling trend among schoolgirls:

> These days there is a proliferation of women who are *not as they should be*.
> Women have been graced with virtue and obedience; their ephemeral language,
> quiet manner, and non-masculine ways are very much what is unique to
> women.... When I hear them talking to their friends, they respond with
> "*boku*" (I) and "*kimi*" (you), and throw in Chinese words. I cannot bear to look
> at their writing when they use Chinese terms in their essays and calligraphy
> practice. They also translate *waka* into Chinese poems. I can say only that they
> have lost their original, pure state. In speech and manner both, it is essential
> that women be *womanly*. Young women learning Chinese words and poetry
> will make themselves ugly.[1]

By depicting *kanbun* (classical Chinese) and its derivative styles as masculine modes of expression and thus unnatural for women to use, comparable
to the use of *Boku* (I) and *kimi* (you), Shihō is lamenting the influence of
Nakajima Shōen (1863–1901)—then known as Kishida Toshiko—whose

popularity as an orator for the Freedom and People's Rights Movement (Jiyū Minken Undō) was shaping discursive trends among young female students. Various anti–Meiji government newspapers lauded Kishida Toshiko as a heroine, but for Shihō, who was writing for the pro-government *Yomiuri*, she was a hindrance to the national project.[2] Shihō believed that for a nation to be strong, women's language should reflect Japanese women's "true nature."[3] But Kishida Toshiko's effect on audiences made it difficult even for pro-government newspaper editors to prevent her from influencing the discursive landscape. By displaying her talent and intellect, and by using language and knowledge derived from classical Chinese, Kishida Toshiko demonstrated that women could speak for reasons other than for appearing beautiful or being obedient, while still retaining a respectable position in society.

A number of historians and literary scholars have written about Kishida Toshiko's importance to the Freedom and People's Rights Movement, women's education, and women's literature in the 1880s. Sharon Sievers has analyzed Toshiko's speeches and essays from 1882 and 1883, noting that Toshiko advocated for women's equal treatment and inspired women to form oratory groups and educational meetings to improve their position in society. Marnie Anderson has shown that Toshiko effectively used her powerful oratory to influence audiences and furthered women's ability to speak forcefully on serious political subjects in public spaces.[4] Rebecca Copeland and Dawn Lawson have examined the importance of Toshiko's novella, *Sankan no meika* (Noble flowers of the mountains), which made waves as part of the mid-Meiji cohort of female writers publishing in *Jogaku zasshi* (Journal for women's learning).[5] These writers experimented with fictional prose that promoted new ways for women's voices to be depicted in fiction.[6] Because this chapter focuses heavily on her *kanshi* (classical Chinese poetry) and diaries, I will hereafter refer to Kishida Toshiko by the name under which she also published her *kanshi* and essays: Shōen.

The desire to define and police the uses of language by educated women like Shōen has existed throughout Japanese history. The newspaper editor Shihō's sentiments have echoes throughout the twentieth century, not just in the late Tokugawa or Meiji eras. Ideas on what was "natural" for a woman to convey in her writing was discussed in a 1908 *zadankai* (roundtable discussion), "On Women Writers," in the journal *Shinchō* (New currents). As Rebecca Copeland explains in the introduction to the translation of this *zadankai*, the male panelists expressed gender-based biases regarding women's desire to write and publish.[7] For example, they expressed irritation at some women writers' "lack of womanliness" and demanded that such writers "take henceforth as their guiding principle the preservation of that within themselves that is most womanly and that they adapt themselves to this womanliness and write accordingly."[8] There appears to have been little improvement in the perception of women's desire to write freely between 1882, when Shihō wrote his opinion piece, and 1908, when the *zadankai* took place. Rather, essays by female authors published in 1908 conveyed a need to respond to the ever-increasing panic over the degree to which women were writing in ways and on subjects outside what male critics defined as "womanly."

Women did not stop writing despite the incessant revulsion rained upon "unwomanly" writers. We see in Yosano Akiko's "What Is 'Womanliness'?" (1921) an understanding of writing as a human act that her fellow women writers had persisted in pursuing: "When women have been liberated from the word 'womanliness,' they will have awakened to their humanity and will no longer be reproductive or cooking puppets. They will be humans and no longer dolls. . . . We need not fear being called 'unwomanly.'"[9] Shōen died in 1901, but it was evident, even at the height of her celebrity, that she, like Yosano, was not fearful of being called "unwomanly," although she took pains to maintain a "respectable" appearance.

The perception that classical Chinese was a language appropriate only for educated, elite men—in other words, that it was unwomanly—was cultivated by some but ignored by talented, privileged women who had been educated in *kanbun* from at least the eighth century. Numerous elite Meiji women received an education in *kanbun*, as is seen throughout this book. An examination of late Tokugawa (ca.1700–1868) attitudes toward *kanbun* reveals that, unlike in the mid-Meiji period, *kanbun* was not perceived exclusively as a component of men's education or only as the language of governance. Historian Martha Tocco notes that Tokugawa-era women with expertise in *kanbun* were not considered "social or educational pariahs."[10] In fact, the prominent neo-Confucian writer Kaibara Ekiken (1630–1714) praised such *kanbun*-literate women as "models of exemplary conduct," even if they were childless, suggesting that women could choose a scholarly life rather than a marital one.[11] Even in the early Meiji period, the gendered division of labor apportioned the teaching of traditional subjects such as *kanbun*, classical Japanese, and calligraphy to educated women, while men were expected to teach "new" knowledge, such as the mathematics and science of the West.[12]

The Kanbunmyaku *of a Meiji Female Social Citizen*

While some of the characteristics of classical Chinese literacy in the early to mid-Meiji period were addressed in the introduction, it is necessary here to examine also the specific aspects that are related to Shōen's training and writing. In the early Meiji period, basic comprehension of classical Chinese text was a skill taught to male and female students through rote memorization. This skill was made available to the educated classes, which included former samurai families as well as merchant and farming families with the resources to send their children to local temple schools. As the notion of a national education system was introduced in the early Meiji period, these older models of local temple schools and tutors gave way to new institutions at both the local and national levels. It is well known that the *genbun itchi* (unification of the written and spoken language) movement homogenized a diversity of expressive styles that existed prior to the mid-Meiji period.[13] Meiji-period writing in these styles, which were replaced by a more accessible, modern, unified language, remains ripe for further analysis, as evidenced by the growing body of literary analyses of Meiji women's use of classical Chinese forms to express their ideas and thereby participate in the discursive marketplace.[14]

Kanbun use in Japan derived from the importation of classical Chinese texts and included the composition of *kanshi* and works written in *kanbun kundokutai* (lit., the style based on [a Japanese] reading of classical Chinese). To address this range of work, Chinese literature scholar Saitō Mareshi has referred to as part of a *kanbun* family, or mode of "styles of [works] with *kanbun*-esque perspectives and sensibilities," which he calls *kanbunmyaku*.[15] *Kanbunmyaku* refers to the sensibilities, knowledge, and philosophies that were imported to Japan through *kanbun* works, as well as those works written by Japanese in the style of *kanbun kundokutai* and *kanshi* and the resulting scholarship and critical tradition. Shōen's readers would have been aware of the depth of education and knowledge required to achieve enough proficiency in *kanbunchō*, a classical Chinese style of prose, to regularly document events in society, incidents occurring within the household, and daily contemplation. Shōen's writings were part of a transformation within the Meiji period in which the uses and cultural meanings of *kanbunmyaku* became entangled in the struggles between the stylistic binaries of masculine and feminine, public and private, and domestic and foreign.

New cultural ideals solidified as the Meiji period progressed, and the early tolerance for *kanbun*-literate women was rescinded as a result of the intentional masculinization of *kanbun* and the feminization of Japan's own literary tradition and national language. Literary scholar Seki Reiko explains that *kanbun* and *kundokutai* came to be identified as masculine styles in the Meiji 20s (mid-1880s to mid-1900s), with the emergence of gender binaries exemplified by terms such as *taoyame buri* (lit., "weak-handed woman" or "graceful" act) and *masurao buri* (lit., "useful rough man" or "heroic" act).[16] According to Seki, this particular binary owes much to the protonationalist *kokugaku* (nativist studies) school of thought, whose leading scholar, Motoori Norinaga (1730–1801), privileged the "quintessentially Japanese" elements of Murasaki Shikibu's *Genji monogatari* (The tale of Genji), which was written in *kana* (Japanese syllabary and prose). In Norinaga's view, the "fabricated and contrived appearances" of contemporary Chinese texts, which characterized much of the official writings of the time, were inferior to the works of Heian-period (794–1185) court women writing in *kana*.[17] As literary scholar Atsuko Sakaki notes, Norinaga equated "femininity with the poetic, the natural, and the indigenous, thus defining it as a quality that needs to be restored in both men's and women's Japanese writing."[18] Norinaga also emphasized the inappropriateness of Chinese as a medium for Japanese writing. His views led to the exclusion of Tokugawa Sinophile women writers from the canon, as opposed to their Heian and medieval counterparts (such as Murasaki Shikibu), "who were viewed as embodying the national identity of Japan."[19] These gender binaries helped shape a national identity that placed value on Japan's native traditions, while viewing those traditions as inherently feminine.

Despite Norinaga's influence, *kanbunmyaku* texts were ubiquitous in Meiji fiction, historical narratives, poetry, and legal pronouncements. Scholar of modern Japanese literature Kamei Hideo describes several other forms of *kanbun*-derived styles that persisted in Meiji-period texts, such as *yakudoku* (translated reading) and *bōyomi* (classical Chinese reading without any markings to assist the reader in determining word order). *Yakudoku* is composed of unannotated lines of Chinese characters reordered to follow Japanese syntax and to incorporate various honorific expressions; it is designed to fit as closely as possible with the parameters of classical Japanese writing. *Bōyomi* "eschewed such [honorific] adjustments and used only a bare minimum of suffixes."[20] Although *kanbun* is considered to be associated either with its official uses or with the classical canon, Kamei (citing Fukuchi Ōchi's "Prose Styles in Present-Day Meiji") suggests that it was not easily composed but was understood: "[For] peasants and townsmen, who wrote on a daily basis in a style that mixed Japanese honorifics into *kanbun* prose, it would not have been difficult to read pure unannotated *kanbun*, even if they could not understand the full corpus of Chinese classical literature."[21] Thus, many readers would have been able to read *kanbun*, whether *bōyomi*, *yomikudashi* (classical Chinese written in Japanese with *kana* word endings and sentence structure), or *yakudoku*. Kamei argues that the removal of honorifics in the *bōyomi* style of *kanbun* allowed characters to emerge as equals in terms of class, gender, and nationality, as in Tōkai Sanshi's *Kajin no kigū* (Chance encounters with beautiful women).[22] Kamei goes so far as to assert that the *bōyomi* style itself, and its strategic use, created a "bridge" linking the author and contemporary readers in a way that would not have been possible with *yakudoku*.[23] Yet despite the leveling of class divisions in such styles as *bōyomi*, the gendering of *kanbun* was becoming more pronounced.

Shōen's *kanbun*-derived, Sinified-Japanese style of writing and speaking—one formed by rendering classical Chinese prose in a way that conveys a grammatical Japanese reading—became a kind of identifying mark for her, both in her own writings and in the descriptions of her published by others. It indicated that she was highly educated, a characteristic that, despite provoking alarm among those who thought it unbecoming to women, benefited her roles as an activist, educator, social critic, and writer. Shōen's *kanbun* style of speech and writing, and the overt display of her skill—that is, her unwillingness to hide or obscure it—elicited criticism simply for being produced by a woman. The discursive world she participated in was in turns fascinated by and threatened by her. In an era of the sexualization of women in public, *kanbun* had the effect of making women "ugly"—as Shihō noted—and might be one reason why Shōen maintained her Sinified style of writing until the end.

The classical Chinese knowledge apparent in Shōen's writing must be understood within the specific conditions of her lifetime. Shōen was not writing about "China" or "Chineseness" when using *kanshi* or *kanbun kun-*

dokutai but was using the form in a way that would have been immediately differentiated by readers from other styles of literacy and learnedness.[24] What was new and startling about Shōen's literacy was that it was on public display and circulated in the press. As the orator Kishida Toshiko in the Freedom and People's Rights Movement, Shōen never hid her *kanbun* literacy in her speeches or her writing, despite the media's insistence on its lack of femininity.[25] In fact, throughout her life she chose to write in a style closer to classical Chinese than classical Japanese, or *genbun itchi* style, even though she was publishing as this modern literary movement emerged. Shōen's publicized and politicized proficiency in classical Chinese reached wider readership because of the readers' continued *kanbun* literacy as well as the growing circulation of contemporary women's writings in print. Thus, Shōen's writing had the subversive potential to inspire young female readers to seek as rigorous an education as possible and to express political ideas. This was aided by the fact that Shōen was among those equipped to participate right away in literary journals as an essayist and poet and was making conscious choices about her self-expression. Her participation came amid constantly shifting conventions brought about by the *genbun itchi* movement and debates surrounding the modernization of written language and women's participation in print.

Shihō's editorial demonstrates how Shōen's language provoked responses within her social, political, and literary context. Russian linguist V. N. Voloshinov explains that "to observe the phenomenon of language, both the producer and the receiver of sound and the sound itself must be placed into the social atmosphere."[26] Shōen's existence in the social and linguistic atmosphere of the 1880s and 1890s Freedom and People's Rights Movement and in literary and women's education discourses created rare but illuminating conflicts in the language, between gender and style of expression or about the degree to which writers could rely on classical Chinese to inform modern prose. What emerged was a combination of new and old practices taking place at once. As a woman educated in classical Chinese within a new but robust Kyoto public educational system, Shōen used her *kanbun* literacy to participate in the Freedom and People's Rights Movement, to engage in women's education and rights, and to write poetry and fiction. By examining how Shōen expressed herself within these social situations through her work, we can understand her audiences' responses to her literary output.

It is worth noting that Shōen's *kanbun* literacy was first initiated by her mother. Shōen's mother, Kishida Taka, began reading *sūtras* (Buddhist scriptures) aloud to her daughter when she was just three years old and exposed her to a wide variety of cultural and intellectual stimuli. Taka developed the young Shōen's theatrical tastes by taking her to *jōruri* (traditional musical theater) performances and sent her to study with a poetry master in her youth.[27]

Throughout Japanese history, and particularly in the late Tokugawa and early Meiji eras, women composed classical Chinese poetry in addition to being able to read *sūtras*. Atsuko Sakaki describes two eighteenth-century female Sinophiles—the historian and fiction writer Arakida Reijo (1732–1806) and the painter, poet, and calligrapher Ema Saikō (1787–1861)—both of whom were experts in literary and poetic Chinese and were welcomed into discursive worlds that had been the domain of men up to that point. According to Sakaki, their cultural mobility was contingent on the degree of their skill and the support they received from their male teachers and peers.[27] In Nakajima Shōen's case, her acceptance by her male peers into a progressive political movement as a public speaker in the 1880s and in literary journals as a poet, essayist, and fiction writer in the 1890s was contingent on her skill in *kanbun* studies, which incorporated classical Chinese poetry, philosophy, history, and translations of Western works. She was a greater target for wider criticism than her Edo predecessors due to the wider reach of the press coverage of her speeches. Of the Sinophilic female literati of the late Tokugawa and early Meiji periods, Shōen is remembered as a key modern figure because of her participation in the Freedom and People's Rights Movement. Through this movement, she found like-minded thinkers among the highly educated elites, and when many of them became officials within the Meiji government, she joined the middle ranks of Meiji political society by joining her husband in his work in the Meiji government. While her membership within the political class was not a direct result of a shared classical Chinese education and literacy, this intellectual foundation of *kanbunmyaku*, which she shared with her husband and his allies, informed the camaraderie and intellectual debates of that circle and empowered Shōen to participate as an equal member—if not politically, at least intellectually.

As discussed in chapter 1, efforts by the imperial advisors in the Meiji government to support classical Chinese education in the form of Confucian studies also sustained the prestige of classical Chinese literacy as a

privileged and specialized skill into the mid-Meiji period. Shōen's participation in the public world of political activism, writing, and social commentary highlights the social distinction demonstrated and sustained by
kanbun literacy and also shows that Shōen enjoyed certain male privileges
in educational, literary, and press circles as a result. This did not change the
fact that her rights were limited as a woman in Meiji society. Her diaries
reveal the ways she responded to the sociopolitical transformations taking
place through and around her.

Shōen's Early Life and Education

Nakajima Shōen was born Kishida Toshi in Kyoto prior to the Meiji Restoration of 1868 and came of age just as changes were introduced in girls' education, compulsory education, and women's place in society. Shōen's parents were Kishida Mohei, a secondhand clothing dealer, and his wife, Taka.
Both were raised in the village of Tomioka, located in present-day Hyōgo
Prefecture. Her merchant-class family origins were humble, although the
Kishida family's financial circumstances flourished after the great Kyoto fire
of 1874 destroyed the first family business. Mohei rebuilt a lucrative business in textile distribution, which provided his family with relative security
and comfort.

The family's merchant background and early financial struggles may
have helped prepare Shōen to manage her household and her husband's
political bid, when she fundraised to amass the wealth required of members
of the first lower house of the Diet.[29] One of Shōen's earliest biographers,
Sōma Kokkō, notes that Mohei was rarely at home during Shōen's childhood, due at first to his travels on business and then to a mistress with
whom he resided for most of Shōen's youth. His absence from the Kishida
family home may have strengthened Shōen's bond with her mother and her
resolve to improve women's status and promote their financial and social
independence from their husbands.[30]

Shōen found early fame as a prodigy (*shindō*) in Kyoto in the 1870s. The
region's vibrant educational climate allowed ambitious and talented girls to
receive some schooling. Meiji state schools were established first in Kyoto
by reorganizing Tokugawa-era *bakufu* schools, such as the schools of medicine (*Igakusho*), Western studies (*Kaiseijo*), and neo-Confucian studies
(*Shōheikō*).[31] The Kyoto school system opened coed primary schools
throughout its districts beginning in 1869, even before the promulgation of

the Education Edict of 1872 (the Gakusei, issued August 8, 1872), which outlined the country's first public school system for the country and which by decree of Emperor Meiji established mandatory primary education for all children.[32] In fact, after the start of the Meiji period, Kyoto was the first city to open girls' schools, called *jokōba*, where students learned sewing, weaving, reading, and writing, but these schools were closed after 1872. Following the Gakusei, the city of Kyoto swiftly designated additional buildings as schools to expand enrollment and held contests for students to test their memorization and recitation of canonical *kanbun* texts. Shōen was an early beneficiary of the Kyoto public school system and one of its most famous products.

Despite that the Gakusei specified that both girls and boys should receive elementary education, schooling for girls was not a priority for the Meiji government, as Margaret Mehl explains.[33] Though not as expansive as general education for boys, the educational methods for girls proliferated in the early Meiji period. Western missionaries, who taught an English-language curriculum, opened many girls' schools in the mid-Meiji period. The first Christian school for girls, Miss Kidder's School (later Ferris Seminary), opened in 1870, and by 1890 there were forty-three Christian boarding schools for girls with a total enrollment of 3,083 students and fifty-six day schools with 3,426 students.[34] Assailed by arguments that such schools failed to prepare girls for marriage and life according to claims of shared traditional Japanese customs, many of the girls' schools that opened in the 1870s were pushed to shut down after anti-Christian and anti-Western sentiments in the 1890s led to the decline in their popularity. But girls' school attendance lagged behind boys' throughout most of the Meiji period, with higher schooling for girls largely neglected.

In 1876, Shōen received top ranking in her region for a recitation exam on the lectures of the *Wen xuan* (Selections of refined literature). Her proficiency in the Chinese classics placed her among the most educated youth in Kyoto even in the 1870s. This achievement was the equivalent of those awarded by *juku*, private academies for higher education, which were prevalent in the Tokugawa period and populated mostly by male teachers and students, largely of the samurai class.[35] Regional testing systems, which were born of education nationalization, gave Shōen the opportunity to demonstrate her academic parity with future male leaders of Kyoto and beyond.[36]

The Kyoto schools' early curriculum during the Meiji period included works in *kanbun kundokutai* and *kanji kanamajiri* (the standard script of written Japanese) that were memorized and recited by students from a young age. Representative works of the era—such as Rai Sanyō's *Nihon gaishi* (Unofficial history of Japan), *Bankoku kōhō* (Law of the nations, a Chinese translation of Wheaton's *Elements of International Law*), Fukuzawa Yukichi's *Seiyō jijō* (State of the West), and the more traditional teachings of Confucius—provided students with shared knowledge, language, and tools to create a new political strategy.[37] Acquired aurally through memorization and recitation, the rhythm and tone of *kanbun kundokutai* were familiar to Meiji youths, although many would have been hard-pressed to write fluently and persuasively in the style, as described above.[38] Additionally, the language of Meiji government edicts and announcements were issued in *kanbun kundokutai*, adding to the prestige of that style of writing.

This education provided the foundation for Shōen's involvement in the Freedom and People's Rights Movement, allowing her to achieve fluency in the language of contemporary political and literary discourse—a discourse largely produced by and circulated among the nation's educated and ambitious men.[39] Shōen achieved an unprecedented social status for a woman of the former merchant class. After demonstrating her calligraphic talents for Imperial Prince Arisugawanomiya Taruhito (1835–95) in 1877 while he was touring educational institutions in the Kyoto area, she was identified as a suitable candidate for service in the Meiji empress' court.[40] Two years later, she was appointed *monji goyō gakari* (a court attendant who specialized in classical Chinese) in the Meiji empress' court; she was the first woman of commoner origin to serve in such a role.[41] Her salary was an impressive fifteen yen per month, which was more than double the monthly salary of a policeman in 1881.[42] Her service as *monji goyō gakari*, which included providing lessons on the works of Mencius (fourth–third century BCE) for the empress, was a new form of public service and employment for a nonaristocratic woman.

In 1881, Shōen resigned from her post after two years of service and embarked on a journey with her mother, Taka, that would seal her place in Japanese history.[43] The two women traveled along the famed Tōkaidō highway, exploring the southern and western regions of Chūgoku, Kyūshū, and Kōchi, which were in the former domains (*han*) that had fought for the downfall of the Tokugawa shogunate. During this journey, Shōen demonstrated her talent for oratory and her desire to be engaged in the issues and concerns of the era. The historian Nishikawa Yūko surmises that, while serving in the empress' court, Shōen became aware of the political and social unrest chronicled daily in the newspapers she read and that she traveled to Kōchi out of curiosity.[44] Along their journey, she and her mother encountered the men of the Risshisha (Society to Establish One's Ambitions), one of the many Kōchi-based political societies that had been the precursors to the Itagaki Taisuke's (1837–1919) Jiyūtō (Liberal Party). While still on her journey, she joined the Freedom and People's Rights Movement as a speaker, traveling with them to various rural areas. During this time she helped to educate audiences and to present the group's critique of the Meiji government's practices, calling for greater participation and opportunities for social citizenship.

Her importance to the movement was evident by April 1882, when Shōen gave a speech titled "The Way of Women" at the inauguration of the Osaka Provisional Political Speech Event. One of the societies calling for a constitution and a representative assembly, the Rikken Seitō (Constitutional Progressive Party), sponsored the event. Many of the events in which Shōen participated gathered large audiences of five hundred to three thousand people, and news reports of these events describe audiences' enthusiastic responses to her speeches and stage presence. She inspired numerous women to join the movement and, in particular, to take up oratory as a form of public self-expression. A notable example is the Okayama Joshi Kōshinkai (Okayama Women's Social Gathering), which formed after Shōen gave several speeches in the region.

The regional newspaper *Kōchi shimbun* reported daily on meetings and events that involved multiple speakers, and Shōen's name appeared regularly. Her schedule, according to newspaper coverage, shows her speaking up to seven times a month and sometimes for several consecutive days.[45] The speech titles alone—including "The Government as the Force [*ten*] over Men, and Men as the Force over Women" (May 13, 1882, at the Okayama Shinmeiza), "Women Cannot But Combine 'the Rigid and the Supple' [*gōjū*]," and "To Endure What Need Not Be Endured, and to Worry about What Need Not Be a Concern: These Are Not the Duties of Women"— reflect her desire to address women's place in society.

Shōen's arrest in October 1882 derailed her career as a public speaker. After giving a speech in Ōtsu, the capital city of Shiga Prefecture, Shōen was jailed for allegedly undermining the authority of the police. At her trial a month later, she was found guilty of giving a political speech illegally and was fined five yen. Shōen returned home after the trial but continued her involvement with the Freedom and People's Rights Movement, albeit less frequently thereafter. Although rural communities continued to organize for more social participation and less use of police force, the promulgation of the Meiji Constitution in 1889 dissipated the immediate political motivation for resistance as elites within the movement were incorporated into the Meiji government as Diet members, leaving laborers and farmers to fend for themselves. As the Meiji government solidified its authority, elites no longer felt an urgent need and had less use for the social citizenship demanded by the less privileged members of society.

Shōen married Nakajima Nobuyuki, who was, at the time they first met, Liberal Party president Itagaki Taisuke's second in command. It was rumored that Shōen and Nobuyuki married for love (*renai kekkon*), a romantic union scandalous at a time for those of Shōen's and Nobuyuki's stature when the custom was to select a partner by way of an arranged marriage through a go-between. He was of *shizoku* (samurai class) origin but in his youth had abandoned his domain of Kōchi in order to join the movement to "repel barbarians" (*jōi*). Serving under the prominent anti-*bakufu* samurai leader Sakamoto Ryōma (1836–67), he fought against Tokugawa forces in the Chōshū domain's naval fleet. This fleet was part of the Kaientai (Naval Auxiliary Force), a trading and shipping company established in 1864 and composed of samurai who had abandoned their domains to fight against the *bakufu*. Boasting access to Western goods and firepower, the Kaientai were an active force in the anti-Tokugawa movement. Following the Meiji Restoration, Nobuyuki served as a representative for Kanagawa Prefecture near Tokyo and was a member of the Chamber of Elders (Genrōin), a national assembly established in 1875. Nobuyuki was a widower with three sons when he met Shōen. His father-in-law, Mutsu Munemitsu (1844–97)—a hero of the Satsuma Rebellion, a leader within the Freedom and People's Rights Movement, and later a prominent statesman in the Meiji government—had befriended Shōen and introduced her to Nobuyuki.

Shōen and Nobuyuki, who registered their marriage in August 1885, had a home in Yokohama and traveled back and forth to Tokyo as Nobuyuki's political status demanded. When the representative assembly established by the Meiji Constitution commenced in 1890, Nobuyuki served as its first Speaker of the Diet. His term was brief, however, as he was ousted from his position when the first assembly was disbanded on December 25, 1891. Nobuyuki chose not to run for the next Diet session in February 1892. Still, he had strong allies within the government, and in 1893 he was appointed resident minister extraordinary and plenipotentiary to Italy. Though the couple feared the physical strain of the arduous voyage on Shōen's already fragile health, they decided to head for Rome. Once there, Shōen contracted tuberculosis, after which Nobuyuki resigned from his post and the couple returned to Yokohama. Upon their return to Japan, Nobuyuki received an appointment to the House of Peers by imperial command. Although the couple withdrew from active public life, Nobuyuki was further promoted in 1896, when he received the title of *danshaku* (baron), making Shōen a baroness. Shōen never recovered from her illness, and Nobuyuki contracted tuberculosis as well. In their final years, they convalesced in the seaside town of Ōiso in Kanagawa Prefecture. Nobuyuki died first, in 1899, while Shōen survived until May 1901 and breathed her last surrounded by her mother, stepsons, students, and servants.

Kanbunmyaku in the Imperial Court and in the Judicial Court

Much of the existing scholarship on Shōen's life and writings focuses on her activities in the Freedom and People's Rights Movement and her contributions to Meiji women's literature and education. What has been difficult to track and also to highlight in Shōen's life is the empowering function that classical Chinese played in her work and how it shaped the last two decades of her literary output. Shōen expressed herself and encountered the world around her through her writing. While the existing body of diaries covers intermittent periods of her life, she kept diaries while also publishing essays, fiction, and poetry in journals. Her writing demonstrates a literary engagement that spanned her entire adult life. Given the limited venues in which she could publish, her extant diaries are a window into how she envisioned herself as a social citizen.

On September 27, 1891, Shōen transcribed into her diary a brief quote from the French psychologist Alfred Binet (1857–1911): "Binet says style (*buntai*) is a person's psyche" (Binē iwaku buntai wa hito no shinri nari).[46] She may have had some exposure to Binet's research on children's memory of prose narratives, and her note hints at her interest in the connection between writing style and identity. Connections between writing style and "the self" had begun to be debated in the Meiji period. The very idea of the proper *buntai* for writers, as well as for the common Japanese person, was in flux still in the 1880s and 1890s. Shōen may have had to consider what her chosen style of writing conveyed to others and how it shaped her understanding of herself. Shōen's writing found readers; her *kanshi*, records, letters, and court testimonies were available in print. The attention she received for her accomplishments did not always lead to favorable outcomes, and she chose to express her objection through writing.

The poem below is undated, but in it Shōen describes the period of her life she spent as *monji goyō gakari* in the empress' court, which took place from 1879 to 1880.

宮中無一事	In the court not an incident occurs
終日笑語頻	All day, laughter is frequent
錦衣滿殿女	Women dressed in finery fill the hall
窈窕麗於春	So beautiful, they are finer than spring

公宮宛仙境	The court is another immortal domain
杳々遠世塵	Deeply secluded, far away from the dust of the world
幸有日報在	Fortunately, there is the daily newspaper
世事棋局新	The worldly affairs and political situations are up to date

一讀愁忽至	On the first read, I am immediately sorrowful
再読淚霑巾	On the second read, tears soak my kerchief
廉士化為盜	Men of honesty are transformed into thieves
富民變作貧	The wealthy are made poor

貧極還願死	Further impoverished, I rather hope for death
臨死又思親	Facing death, I also think of intimate ones
盛衰雖在命	Although one's rise and fall depends on fate
誰能不酸辛	Who can't but endure hardship

請看明治世	Please look at this Meiji world
不讓堯舜仁	The virtue [of the Meiji emperor] is not second to Yao and Shun's[47]
怪比堯舜政	It is doubtful to claim that [Meiji] rule is comparable to Yao and Shun's
未出堯舜民	The people have not yet risen above Yao and Shun's[48]

Here Shōen describes the "immortal" imperial court and the other finely dressed court women, in contrast to the "dust" conveyed in the newspapers delivered daily for court members to read. The final stanza suggests a political critique, with "Meiji" standing in for the imperial court or possibly the cabinet members. The court women with access to news were in a position to compare the world of the court with what was taking place beyond its walls. But the poet wonders why people (*min*) who would help create an ideal world have not yet risen up. When Shōen went on to join the Freedom and People's Rights Movement between 1882 and 1883, she was able to join the *min* amid "the dust of the world" in a dramatic call for reform and representation.

Shōen's first published poems were written during her time in the Freedom and People's Rights Movement and born out of her brief incarceration in a Shiga jail in 1883. As mentioned earlier, on October 12, following her speech entitled "Hakoiri musume" (Daughters in boxes), Shōen was arrested, incarcerated, and tried on suspicion of violating the Public Gatherings Ordinance of 1880 (*shūkai jōrei ihan*) for giving a political speech in Ōtsu despite having only a permit for an educational speech and for contempt of the police (*kanri bujoku zai*).[49] On the day of her arrest, rather than interrupt Shōen's speech—which was the most common and effective way to obstruct a political rally—the police had the speech transcribed in its entirety. After she completed her speech and the crowd dispersed, Shōen was apprehended as she and her students were leaving the theater. The manner of her arrest indicates that the police wanted to avoid immediate publicity and the possibility of provoking an outcry from her audience.[50] Led to the local precinct, Shōen was placed in a cell. Although several newspapers reported that one of her students, the eight-year-old Tachi Fuji, pled tearfully with the police chief to release her because of her fragile health, Shōen was refused bail.[51] Ten days later she was released into the custody of her older brother, Renzaburō.[52]

The following stanzas are excerpted from a series of poems that appear to have been composed during Shōen's incarceration. This poem, which begins with a *shichigon risshi* (seven-character octastich), is followed by three stanzas of *gogon zekku* (five-character quatrains), repeats another *shichigon risshi*, and ends with twenty-two seven-character lines:

假令吾如蠖曲身	Even though my body bends like an inchworm
胸間何屈此精神	In my heart is a spirit that will yield to nothing
雨聲無是母親淚	The voice of the rain, is it not my mother's tears
情殺獄中不寐人	One cannot sleep as imprisonment kills passion
母在客中兒獄中	My mother stays as a guest, her child is in jail
愁雲恨雨意將窮	Sad clouds, resentful rains; my will almost expended

寒燈不照夜如歳　The cold lamp emits no light, night feels like a year
羨殺遙天秋一鴻　I am exceedingly envious of the autumn goose that drifts in the sky

身論道義繁刑縲　I spoke of human rights and was bound by police
正是明治文化時　Truly this is the era of Meiji cultural enlightenment
輪月多情故穿枕　The full moon with much passion pierces my pillow
寒風薄意痛砭肌　The cold wind without feeling painfully stabs my skin

人言政體不如刻　People say that a government is not so cruel
何事民間切唱悲　Then of what do the people ceaselessly cry out
軟骨亦能馴世昧　My pliant body has become used to the ways of the world
獄中高臥賦吟詩　So that in prison, my pillow raised, I compose poetry[53]

The poem begins with Shōen's enduring concern for the well-being of her mother, Taka. But this concern did not dampen her ire nor weaken her will to lament her unjust incarceration (胸間何屈此精神). The moonlight struck her pillow and the wind lashed at her skin as she lay awake (雨聲, 愁雲恨雨, 寒風, 穿枕, 砭肌). She was battered by the cold and wind, yet despite her discomfort, her language was defiant (何屈、道義、高臥). Refusing to yield to despair, she invoked a classical image of a government that needs no violence to enforce its just will. Shōen referred derisively to the "Meiji *bunka*," that is, the Meiji culture touted by her government (正是明治文化時). With the poet in the grip of emotion, her world seems bound tightly by the fixed structure of the lines and likewise by the restrictive walls of her cell, perforated by nature and injustice alike.

Due to the government's growing concerns over the participation of women at political events, the Public Gatherings Ordinance explicitly included women among a diverse group of individuals who were barred from joining political parties and attending political gatherings, although women could still gather if the event was educational in nature. The historian Ōki Motoko explains that specific policies for restricting women's political activities were previously permitted, but they were enforced at the discretion of the police.[54] A police chief or attending officer could simply deem a woman's presence at the podium "a threat to public safety" (*chian ni bōgai ari*) to justify terminating a gathering or arresting the speaker and venue owner. Furthermore, in 1882 various newspapers published a rumor that the police chief in Ōtsu categorically denied all of the applications for permits to give political speeches submitted by women and by men under twenty years of age. The police's heightened security measures were a direct response to Shōen's shocking popularity.[55]

Yet as research on the relationship between the press and criminal trials in the mid-Meiji period has shown, the press jumped at the chance to cover Shōen's arrest. In an effort to assuage the public's anxiety over new judicial practices, the government began to permit open trials in 1872. It was for this reason that a transcription of "Daughters in Boxes" was the only one of Shōen's speeches to survive. The transcription used at the trial was pre-served as part of the *Ōtsu jiken kōhan bōchō hikki* (Ōtsu incident public trial transcript), which was serialized in the *Rikken Seitō shimbun* (Pro-Constitution Party newspaper). The paper had a vested interest in covering the trial, for Shōen had served as a consultant for the publication prior to her arrest.[56]

During the trial, Shōen's experience as a public speaker served her well. The newspaper's publication of her testimony helped disseminate her cri-tique of the police's actions. It was a *Rikken Seitō* reporter who transcribed the trial, which took place in the Shiga Misdemeanor Court at 10:00 a.m. on November 12, 1883, exactly a month after Shōen's arrest. At the time of the arrest, Shōen was a star of the Freedom and People's Rights Movement, helping to draw crowds for events featuring five to ten speakers. But as a woman, her arrest and incarceration had the potential to mar her reputa-tion.[57] In the transcript of the trial published by the *Rikken Seitō* newspaper, Shōen emerged as a sympathetic, politically victimized figure. According to the newspaper's report, after Shōen's speech was read aloud by the clerk, the judge asked for her confirmation of its accuracy. Despite Shōen's harrowing ten-day prison stay after her arrest, her response was a calm and articulate rejection of the charges against her:

> I [*jibun*] have in the past given educational speeches according to the permit application submitted, and did not give a political speech [when granted a per-mit for an educational speech]. . . . But that night, I was of the mind to give an educational lecture exclusively on women's education, thus I did not apply for a permit to give a political speech. Therefore to be charged in this manner is for the defendant highly extraordinary and cannot be described as anything but a tremendous outrage [*meiwaku senban*]. I think the prosecutor has only taken at face value [*saishin*] what the reporting officer described, according to his imag-ination. During the speech, when I spoke of "freedom this" and "freedom that,"

it was a discussion of moral freedom [*dōtokujō no jiyū*] and was in no way about political freedom [*seijijō no jiyū*]. In other words, I analyzed the duties of parents and of women and lamented the bad customs of past educational practices for women. . . . I had no intention [*oboenashi*] of going beyond the framework of women's education, nor did I give a political speech or insult the police. Therefore, there is no reason for me to be the defendant in this prosecution.[58]

Shōen testified from an unwavering position of blamelessness, forcefully articulating her opinion of the arrest. She instructed the court on the mistaken views of the prosecution, going so far as to accuse the prosecutor of simply adopting the language of the transcription. In defending herself, Shōen demonstrated a kind of social citizenship, which was rooted in suffrage and a belief in moral freedom and differed from the citizenship afforded to men of wealth. Her assertiveness is notable given that she lacked suffrage. But owing to the publication of her testimony, her social citizenship was put on full display for the public. Protesting the police's practice of arbitrary arrest as an act of censorship, Shōen in her defense conveys an authority and a self-assurance that was unusual among female defendants covered in the press.

Literary scholar John Mertz explains that in this period public opinion and salacious media coverage had the potential to "upstage" the more sensational criminal trials of the period. In the instance of Shōen's case, the press helped determine popular opinion about her case before the court rendered its verdict. This was in part due to the government's efforts to show the openness of the court process, which in turn allowed the public to have a "rich knowledge of ongoing court cases before the government was able to conclude them."[59] While Mertz writes specifically about the narratives that arose from these public court cases, his observation about the relationship between the government and the people is relevant to the serialized accounts of Shōen's trial: "The configuration of the documentary narratives was fully consonant with an age in which the position of the people versus the government had yet to be decided . . . and equally, in which the position of the nation itself in the international order had yet to be determined."[60] Indeed, Shōen's trial allowed readers to imagine a society in which women would be able to question the authority of the misguided police, as well as the court that found her guilty.

Considering the speech "Daughters in Boxes" in the context of the trial that made it famous, we see that the trial helped to highlight changes in social relations that mirrored the demands of the Freedom and People's Rights Movement. As the historian Barbara Molony notes, the women's movement in this period sought merely the inclusion of women in society, not yet a revolution.[61] The trial itself was a public battle of interpretations in which Shōen presented a series of unusual literary and political metaphors that juxtaposed women with politics. The media coverage of her confrontation with the police and the judiciary system was yet another forum in which Shōen could perform as an empowered female defendant. Her testimony tested the gendered limits of a still-transitioning legal system. In the process, Shōen was immortalized as a heroine and became something of a martyr of the Freedom and People's Rights Movement, even though this was not the kind of fame she sought. While her defense rested on her claim that her speech was apolitical and incorrectly transcribed, the narrative of her direct confrontation with her accusers dramatized a woman's direct challenge to the state.

Shōen Nikki, the Kanbunchō Diaries of 1903

As mentioned earlier, Nakajima Shōen's diaries were written in *kanbunchō*, a classical Chinese style of prose. A portion of her extant diaries was first published under the title *Shōen nikki* in 1903, a little over a year after her death.[62] These *kanbunchō* diaries are a record of the thoughts of a *kanbun*-educated woman writing at the turn of the twentieth century, of which few other examples exist or have been examined. The diaries are part of the emergence of the modern, educated Meiji woman and display a proud and critical perspective that provoked men like Katō Shihō to criticize the content as unfeminine. The currently published volumes of Shōen's diaries cover almost a decade, spanning from September 13, 1891, through May 20, 1901, several days before her death. The notebooks that remain are a fraction of the approximately sixty notebooks that Shōen's mother, Taka, had in her possession upon Shōen's death. Most were destroyed after her death at Shōen's behest.[63]

The two final volumes of Shōen's diaries, which were penned just before her death in 1901, were first published under the title *Shōen nikki* (Shōen diaries) in 1903. In November 1902, aspiring novelist Fujii Tei traveled by train from Tokyo to Ōiso to meet with Taka and request any remaining unpublished works that she might have preserved since her daughter's death a year earlier. Fujii, who would go on to publish a novel and a collected biography of great Japanese women in English, wanted to preserve Shōen's writings while memories of her were still fresh and her unpublished writings were still available. These later diaries, from the period of Shōen's convalescence from tuberculosis and heart disease in Ōiso, from 1899 to 1901, were handed over to Fujii. A year later, in 1903, *Shōen nikki* was published with a selection of Shōen's classical Chinese poems and miscellaneous essays.

Upon reading the 1903 *Shōen nikki* collection, critics were divided in their responses. Shortly after the diary's publication, several newspapers and journals offered favorable reviews. Reviewers disagreed, however, on which era Shōen belonged to. Was she of "this era" (*tōsei*), as the reviewer known as Seigan (Blue Eyes) suggested in the journal *Jokan* (Paragon of womanhood), or was she a heroine of the "recent past" (*kinsei*), as stated in the *Kyōiku jikkenkai* (Education experiment group)?[64] Some found Shōen's example inspiring, noting her "abundant fighting spirit" (*kachiki manpuku*), "refined warm-heartedness" (*onga kankō*), and "virginal solemnity" (*shojoteki shinsotsu*).[65] The *Asahi shimbun* called on "those ladies who think only of their home life and of nothing else" to read *Shōen nikki* to find more interests beyond their domestic duties.[66] Others admired Shōen's refined language, "exceptional" (*idai*) knowledge, and "nonconforming" (*kikei*) perspective and described her tone and viewpoints as unusual for a woman.[67] Labeling the unfamiliar as unique and unusual indicated an inability or lack of desire to place Shōen's life, writing style, or perspective within the context of life in the Meiji period.

One reviewer in particular noted the contradictory effect Shōen's diary had on her readers. On May 10, 1903, Tokutomi Sohō (1863–1957), founder of the Min'yūsha (People's Friend) publishing company and editor of Japan's first general-audience magazine, *Kokumin no tomo* (Friend of the nation), published an extensive and critical review of *Shōen nikki* in the Sunday edition of the *Kokumin shimbun* (Nation's newspaper).[68] In his review, "*Shōen nikki o yomu*" (Reading *Shōen nikki*), Sohō reluctantly admitted that "as literary language, the prose is incredibly close to ideal."[69] To assure his readers that he was an objective critic, he referred back to his days as a young reporter in the early 1880s, when he resisted Shōen's celebrity as an orator. He had, he claims, avoided her well-publicized speeches when other newsmen had flocked to hear her.[70] Yet when he read her diary, he was convinced that Shōen was "above the norm of Meiji women," that her knowledge and refinement were exceptional, and that she was courageous and calm in the face of her debilitating illness; she was, he asserts, "clearly unlike normal women." He adds, however, that Shōen "lacks the qualities unique to women, such as compassion and seriousness."[71] Showing more concern with her lack of femininity than with her writing, he states: "The severity of [her] critical eye and her attention to detail lead to an unfortunate loss of those feminine qualities that are loved in women; even with her exceptional qualities, [she] leaves much to be desired."[72] Sohō thus transitions smoothly from reviewing Shōen's writing to questioning her womanliness. He concludes that she is excessively critical and overly detailed, accusations that are not fully supported by the diaries. As a result, he finds her to be an incomplete woman, exceptional only in her learning and writing, and an undesirable woman, even though her diary is a work of "ideal prose."[73]

Sohō advocated for liberal democracy and populism throughout the 1870s and 1880s, but he became an avid nationalist and imperialist after Western powers forced Japan to territory won in the Sino-Japanese War of 1894–95. Sohō supported a Meiji oligarchy that he had fiercely criticized a decade earlier. In Sohō's nationalistic analysis, Shōen's writing failed to play the proper role within the national imagination, which was one of the inspirations for Japanese literature of this period.[74] Pro-war propaganda leading into the Sino-Japanese War steered the national imagination toward militarism and public masculinity. Furthermore, when promoters of a "national spirit" and national literary tradition began to focus on the legacy of Heian women writers, women's writing in general came to be read as a reflection of the writer's character—an assumption that Sohō seems to be working under in his review of Shōen nikki. This perspective on national literature and culture did not exclude female writing per se but instead allowed only certain kinds. Shōen's writings were excluded from the national canon by failing to account for "the male gaze" that female writers were expected to keep in mind. In this way, by demonstrating some "lack," Shōen's diaries compelled Sohō to clearly articulate how he believed women writers should behave and write.

Not all reviewers interpreted Shōen's "unfeminine" approach as a negative aspect of her style, though some perpetuated other gender stereotypes. Jokan's reviewer stated that "the pathos gushing forth from [Shōen's poetry] is unlike a woman's" (kansō hittan ni hashirite, hotondo nyonin no shi to omowarezu). Fujin shimbun's reviewer asked, "[With] the ease of her brush, the manly [otokorashii] tone, magnanimous sensibility, and the calm manner in which she delivers wit, who would not be surprised that this emerged from the brush of a woman, a tubercular patient who may not even live to see another day?"[75] The divisive effect that *Shōen nikki* had on its reviewers also indicates how standards for women's behavior and writing were still in flux. Shōen's writing was evaluated as either beneficial or harmful to its readers, depending on whether a given reviewer valued work by a woman who refused to write "naturally."

Shōen's diaries and poetry are a prism through which to explore the relationship between her written language and her perceptions of the social and literary worlds for which she wrote. Her diaries display a distinctly authorial voice that explains and justifies her desire to participate as a thoughtful member of society. They are proof that from 1891 until the day of her death she remained actively interested in politics, current events, and culture. She was better able to stay at the forefront of political debates in the early 1890s, when Nobuyuki was Speaker of the Diet, but her practice of reading newspapers and interacting with visitors shows that she sought after knowledge even in her later years. The diary is a record of her responses as a consumer of news as well as an enthusiastic social citizen who was well aware of the restrictions on her rights and their injustice.

Given Shōen's limited mobility during the last years of her life, the earlier notebooks she kept before her illness provide a contrast through records of Shōen's encounters with the outside world. A number of these earlier diary notebooks surfaced in 1986, when *Shōen nikki* was republished along with previously unpublished diary content obtained by the historian Nishikawa Yūko from a descendant of Shōen. This unpublished content comprised two additional notebooks from 1891 to 1892, which were written during Nobuyuki's tenure as the first Speaker of the lower house of Parliament. During this time, Shōen and Nobuyuki hosted numerous political acquaintances, party members, and former activists at their home, including Foreign Minister Mutsu Munemitsu and Prime Minister Itō Hirobumi and his wife.[76] These entries richly describe developments in the Diet, requests to Shōen for introduction letters and tickets to sit in the Diet gallery, and a running record of gifts sent by friends and family members. Shōen and Nobuyuki were at the center of a busy hive of political activity in the first years of the Diet.

The newly minted lower house of Parliament (Shūgiin) was a space where Shōen could practice social citizenship. By attending the parliamentary sessions, Shōen was an observer but could cause a stir with her presence by reminding the male politicians of women's explicit exclusion from their ranks.

In October 1890, the Regulations of the House of Representatives prohibited women from sitting in the galleries. Thus her right to sit to observe Diet proceedings was only made possible on December 3, 1890, when the law barring women from the gallery was overturned after Shimizu Toyoko (or Shikin, 1868–1933) successfully argued that this law violated women's rights.[77]

Shōen regularly attended parliamentary sessions despite, or perhaps because of, the commotion her presence created. As an outsider with no legal rights of her own, she was intruding on the space of governance run by "legitimate" male participants. The *Kokumin shimbun* (Nation's newspaper) reported on one such visit on November 29, 1891, as follows:

> Yesterday morning at No. 2 reception, Representatives' salaries (half) and travel allowances were distributed. Two women approached the desk together, asking to see Secretary Sone. The guard appeared to be saying, "Can the likes of a woman even be permitted a meeting [with the Secretary]?" [*Onna datera ni menkai mo yoku dekita' to iwanu yurushi no fū nite*], but before he could respond, former Liberal Party member Ozaki [Yukio] came by. Seeing these woman, [Ozaki] corrected his posture and informed the guard that this was Speaker Nakajima's wife, Shōen *joshi*. She told the guard that she was there in her husband's place to pick up his salary. At last, the guard understood and, blushing, apologized for his rudeness. It is said that the woman with her was Kageyama [Fukuda] Hideko.[78]

The newspaper reporter emphasizes the tension in the exchange between Shōen and the guard, adding inferences that emphasize the latter's derisive stance by referring to her and Fukuda Hideko as "*onna datera*" (lit., "though only women"). Ozaki refers to Shōen using *joshi*, an honorific reserved for female scholars. The guard's behavior is corrected only in reference to Shōen's husband's status as the Speaker, although the press and readers would have been familiar enough with Shōen *joshi* herself.

Shōen's diary, by contrast, records the encounter more matter-of-factly: "28th Sunny. In the morning, Setooka and Nakamura visited. [Later] I went to the Parliament . . . as I had one more errand to take care of. The guard was extremely haughty. This made me even more polite. Then I met with the Secretary."[79] It is only the next day, when *"Jiji tsūshinsha* [Times dispatch newspaper] sent a handful of articles," that Shōen acknowledges the public nature of the encounter: "29th. ... The [newspaper] page is adorned with all that happened yesterday at the Parliament building. This is truly an annoying situation [*jitsu ni urusaki kotodomo nari*]."[80] The articles Shōen received make much of the confrontation between the guard and the women's rights activists he sought to bar from the parliamentary building. Newspaper reporters repeated the phrase that Shōen and Hideko were "mere women." Though Shōen may have submitted to laws enforcing public order and social cohesion, she refused to cede spaces of political governance that were legally permitted to women by continuing to sit in the women's gallery. Furthermore, she refused simply to internalize the sexist insults. In her diary, she writes that she was undaunted the following day when, on November 31, 1891, she attended a lower house session to hear a speech given by Itō Hirobumi on "the state of administrative policies, the advantages of the current minister, and what the state of affairs should be in the lower house of Parliament":

> If I sat in the gallery, I knew that it would appear in all the newspapers, but this [experience] is a form of education. Fortunately, this year there are gallery seats for women, so I thought to have a look. I walked up to the entrance of the gallery ten minutes before one o'clock. The guard recognized me so he kindly guided me to the women's seats. Several hundred spectators turned their eyes in my direction. The women's seats were right above the newspaper reporters' seats. Among the reporters, there were some who knew me, and we nodded in greeting.[81]

Her presence caused a stir among the reporters seated just below the female visitors' seating area, yet she refused to allow this exclusion to prevent her from observing the proceedings.[82]

In her diary entry for December 21, 1891, Shōen expressed excitement that she would be able to attend a session in which Naval Minister Kabayama Sukenori (1837–1922) excoriated the lower house for objecting to the government's expansion of the navy. The heated debate indicated the resistance of ruling-class authorities to sharing power with those below them. Kabayama later commanded the landing forces on Taiwan, after it was ceded to Japan through the Treaty of Shimonoseki, and became governor general there. He was vehemently opposed to representative government and drew the ire of the lower house members with his open insults. Shōen writes on December 21, 1891:

> Today's Diet had to be seen firsthand, and not read about after the fact. Even if the meeting minutes had recorded every word without mistake, even if news reporters had covered the scene inside and out, I would still feel dissatisfied. How happy I am that I obtained a gallery seat today! The news reporters may have mocked me for smiling at the Speaker's [Nakajima Nobuyuki] perfor-mance on the house floor and things of that sort, but they could not ruin my enjoyment of seeing it all to the end. The naval captain Kabayama climbed up to the podium and easily dismissed [concerns about] the budget problem; and just as he tried to shove out of the sumo ring the proposal for an appraisal [by the members of Parliament], the topic shifted completely to Sugita Sadakazu's proposal for the imperial address.[83]

Shōen's reference to the sumo ring is intended to mock Kabayama's dra-matic performance on the house floor by comparing it to a sumo match. Kabayama's speech was especially critical of civilian involvement in govern-ment decisions. As Speaker of the house, Nobuyuki repeatedly rang the floor bell to halt the speech, but even with protests drowning him out, the naval minister persisted.[84] The second Diet session was dissolved shortly thereafter by the Meiji emperor on December 25, 1891, after the house sought to temper the power of the elites by voting down the bill to support railroad expansion.

As an opponent of representative government, Kabayama was an enemy of the very ideals that Shōen had fought for in the Freedom and People's Rights Movement. She writes about him with a tone of amusement, but it was likely a bitter frustration that she had no right to argue against him at the Diet podium. Shōen's perspective was that of a marginal yet socially respected member of society, but it was one more privileged than her fe-male readers enjoyed themselves. It was through her eyes that a woman might have imagined asserting her own views on the Diet floor. As Shōen herself wrote, a successful women's movement is impossible without ordi-nary women resisting their societal restrictions.[85] Seeming almost to have returned to the role of an "ordinary woman," Shōen writes from the gallery, preparing for a future in which women would be speaking on the Diet floor alongside men.

When the Speaker got notification of the Meiji emperor's dismissal of the second Diet on December 25, 1891, Shōen transcribed it word for word in her diary.[86] In the wake of this imperial overruling of uncooperative political representatives, Shōen recorded an exchange with Nobuyuki on December 31, 1891. Lamenting the corrupt government's bribery of local mayors and officials when she herself was denied a full seat at the table, Shōen quotes herself as saying:

> "I do not care that the government seeks to create a government party and compete with the Liberal Party for the third Diet session, but how hideous of them to use bribes, police pressure, and secret influence over regional mayors and town leaders." To this *kimi* [Nobuyuki] smiled and said, "My dear, listen to me calmly. Society has never been refined and pure. Believing this intently, and then being astounded by the government's payment of bribes, or shocked that a gentleman of the people is tainted by corruption, would cause one to lose all courage to go out into society. . . . The Diet is a playground. If you want children to play there, you must also join them. But you cannot allow them to play willy-nilly. You must establish an order; assert what to do this time and what to do next. If one ends up calling it child's play, and then uses that as a reason not to participate, then one should never have demanded a representative body to begin with."

Both Nobuyuki and Shōen, who actively sought a representative body in the Meiji government, had to adapt to the limitations of the bicameral parliamentary system, which was in flux and riddled with corruption in its early years.

Shōen's engagement with public events as merely an observer situated her as an outsider, despite her extensive knowledge of contemporary issues. She narrates her public performance as a marginalized yet self-aware societal participant, a privilege that was rare for women of this period, during which women experienced limited access to discursive spaces for their intellectual, psychological, and political cultivation. We might view Shōen's diary entries as a testimony—an articulate defense of her actions and her presence in a given context—that produced the conditions requiring a testimony that would otherwise go unheard.[87] Thanks to her ability to give her own account of her life in the world, we see a view of a woman in public who repeatedly challenged standards of femininity for women's language and behavior.

One of the diary notebooks that were recovered in the 1980s contains entries from the last two months of 1893, when Nobuyuki was appointed resident minister extraordinary and plenipotentiary to Italy and the two prepared for their long journey and residence abroad. Shōen has already
indicated concern over her fragile health and writes of her family's fear that
she might not survive the trip to Italy. These entries allowed Shōen to leave
behind a narrative of what the opportunities for travel and writing meant to
her.

Shōen's account of a ball to celebrate Nobuyuki's appointment to the
position in Italy contrasts the pomp and honor of such an appointment to
the risk of a long sea voyage on Shōen's health. Shōen describes the event as
a reluctant but observant guest who is uncomfortable and detached from
the festivities. On November 3, 1892, alongside several other dignitaries,
Shōen and her husband attended the Minister of Foreign Affairs' Ball,
which was hosted by the then minister of foreign affairs, Mutsu Munemitsu—
Nobuyuki's former brother-in-law and a close friend of Shōen. With amusement at the finery and splendor, Shōen observes the grand event:

> Over a thousand attended. The castle was lit up as if to say that even night could
> not contend with it, and was bereft of shade under the glare of the electric lights;
> light shone on beauties who were [already] at their most striking and luminous.
> Old ladies who might be called "Grandmother" were covered in snow-white
> powder, exposing their collarbones and décolletage. Ladies who may have once
> moved about freely, working in their kitchens, now seemed unable to walk a
> single step without help. Grasping onto a man's hand for every step, each one
> made her way into the ballroom. After a while, music struck up in one corner
> of the room. Angels opened their silken fans with their slender hands, flowers
> gracing their necklines. How many worked to sew [that] black gown with gold
> stripes? Several handsome men paired up with their partners and began to
> dance. I was there and, considering it somewhat ludicrous, sat staring for about
> three songs. Imagining the rest of the party's program would follow along these
> lines, I thought it pointless to sit on this cold night with my throat exposed.
> While I wanted to say a word to my husband before I left, I could not find him.
> So I had no choice but to slip out and go home. The experience of changing
> one's clothes and lying down to sleep was a joy beyond measure.[88]

This account is a stark contrast to the coverage of the event in the *Yomiuri shimbun*, which celebrated the event's elegance. An article from Novem-

ber 5 begins with a long list of government officials and their wives, on which Minister Nakajima and his wife appear last. It then notes that fashion trends are moving away from Western ball gowns, with "many more ladies than last year wearing traditional Japanese dress,"[89] adding that kimono-clad ladies who had chosen not to wear a Western ball gown had to wait in chairs alongside the ballroom as those who were dressed more appropriately for the event danced with their partners. The evening's highlight, according to the article, was the attendance of two women from the imperial family who were led into the ballroom by the foreign minister and prime minister.[90] A lavish dinner was provided, with the royalty seated separately from the others, after which dancing commenced again and ended only at two o'clock in the morning.

A Diary Written for Other Women

Shōen records such public events alongside intimate and mundane exchanges that take place in her home. Like Fujii Tei, who sought out Shōen's diaries after her death in order to publish them, Shōen's female students and admirers perpetuated her memory and interest in her work. They continued to visit her throughout the last decade of her life and looked to her as a female role model, someone who appeared to transcend the restrictions placed on women in Meiji society. Shōen seemed aware of her relative privilege and of the frustrating barriers other women faced. In her diary, she observed their struggle but was unable to improve their lives directly.

Shōen could be as critical of her female companions as she was of the world at large, and she cultivated connections with women through frank exchanges. The fluidity with which her public wit was directed to her private interactions defied how women were often depicted in literary and media narratives of the time. Toward her cousin Satoko, Shōen showed maternal care: on the occasion of her wedding, she wrote up a marital handbook that included guidance on a wide array of subjects including sewing, cooking, reading, calligraphy, and mathematics—all things deemed essential to the housewife.[91] This was in spite of the fact that Shōen was not one to abide by the traditional Confucian seven principles (Three Obediences and Four Virtues). According to the family lore passed down through Shōen's mother, Taka, the failure of her first marriage shortly after leaving the imperial court was supported by a letter from her in-laws, who listed which of the principles Shōen had failed to observe. That she could prepare her own manual indicated that she was well versed in the language of the conventions of marriage and the conditions under which women lived, and she understood that such a guide could serve as a tool for survival.

Another younger woman whom Shoēn mentored is Sakazaki (née Nakamura) Toku, a fellow female orator in the Freedom and People's Rights Movement. They both gave speeches on October 2, 1883, at the Kyoto Shijō Hoken Gekijō, ten days prior to Shoēn's arrest; Toku's speech was titled "Is a Woman's Responsibility Heavy or Light?" (*Joshi no nin wa hatashite omokika karukika*).[92] On December 3, 1891, Shoēn describes a visit from Toku:

> Sakazaki's wife visits. Our talk always returns to the Meiji 10s. Every time we meet we repeat the same things; we laugh where we always laugh, pause where we always pause. She still does not call me Madame [*Okusama*], but Teacher [*Sensei*] instead. After a while, out of habit I call her Nakamura or I call her by her first name. It is amusing how we can pretend that we are both still unmarried [*dokushin*].[93]

The diaries also reveal that because Shoēn and Nobuyuki were better off financially than some of their Freedom and People's Rights Movement compatriots, former students and fellow activists like Fukuda Hideko would write requesting donations to help start a school for girls. Likewise, Toku, who was married to journalist and former Liberal Party member Sakazaki Shiran (1853–1913), would write to request the occasional loan from Shoēn.[94] Shoēn makes note of these requests and in the case of Toku lamented her friend's struggle.

Throughout the diaries and in the records of her travels before her marriage, Shoēn's most steady companion was her mother, Taka. We see her quiet wisdom comfort Shoēn, who wrote lovingly of their exchanges. In her biography of Shoēn, Sōma Kokkō describes Taka as the daughter of a *sake* merchant who possessed strong calligraphic skills and who demonstrated a deep knowledge of the Buddhist *sūtras* and a strong devotion to Nichiren Buddhism.[95] According to Sōma, Taka's calligraphy was "bold" (*nikubuto*) and thus reflected a masculine personality, much like her daughter's pieces, several of which still hang in a number of homes and community centers in the Kansai region.[96] Perhaps the most remarkable aspect of Shoēn's upbringing were the pilgrimages she and Taka made together on foot while Shoēn was still a child, with stops to paint the landscapes, write poetry, and produce works of calligraphy, which were offered as gifts to people befriended along the way. Among their arduous pilgrimages, they traveled twice to the temple on Mount Nachi in Wakayama Prefecture, a challenging journey favored by literary pilgrims.[97]

On February 22, 1894, Shōen describes an incident in which a mother and daughter must be separated for some time and is reminded of just such a parting with her own mother:

> Long ago when I was still serving in the imperial court, I met with my mother, who came to visit me. I obtained a two to three hour break and walked with her through the gardens and along the trees in full autumn colors. Sharing a bench, we told each other tales. Even while our time together was ending, our talk would not cease. I think it was because we hated to part.[98]

Both Taka and Shōen were literate in classical Chinese, albeit in different fields within the *kanbun* canon: Taka studied religious texts while Shōen focused on the classics and poetry. The importance of this shared interest and mode of expression was evident even in their most difficult conversations. On October 31, 1891, Shōen writes of the following exchange with her mother:

> It is not that I never dreamed of breathing the air of Europe. But now that I am destined to go, I think of my two parents who are of old age. This being the case, I may regret not delaying this trip. Having no clear answer for what to do, I wished to discuss it with my dear mother [*bokō*] before deciding, and told her all my thoughts. With a serious expression on her face, she said solemnly, "You have a duty to carry out, have you not? Time flies like a waving shuttle and good opportunities are hard to get [歳月如梭好機易得]. I will protect this household while you are away." Hearing Mother's words, my choice was clear. Not to doubt—that is my nature. From tomorrow I will settle any remaining business and concentrate on packing our clothes. Those who know of my weak health have warned against my going as it would surely shorten my life, asserting that I would never return.
>
> It is not as though I did not have these thoughts myself. . . . If I were to die before Mother, what would she do? It was impossible to know, but I wished to know, and so obliquely I said: "Mother, longevity is not what makes a human fortunate. Those who achieve a name for themselves do not worry about where they will die." She answered, "I am of the same mind," and so I was somewhat comforted. If a stranger read this, they might laugh at the immense sacrifice

with no gain. My strength, however, is in feeling things intensely and encountering things lightly. All in all, the love that has developed along this long journey between my mother and me is something that a stranger could not even fathom.[99]

Taka's encouragement to her to choose duty and to remain ambitious gave Shōen the strength to take paths she might otherwise eschew. As seen in this subdued yet intense exchange, Shōen describes her heartfelt communications with her mother in *kanbun* and *kanshi*. Her decision might mean an eternal separation, yet Taka understands Shōen's desire to see the world and not shy away from action and participation in the world.

On November 29, 1892, before departing for Italy, Shōen composed the following two verses to express the various feelings that had arisen due to the impending journey:

> The days may flow like water
> But four springs and autumns will not pass quickly,
> The sounds of insects in the autumn garden, rain outside the spring window
> Will they not make my mother miss this house?
>
> The grief of the one who stays behind is the same as that of the one who
>   departs
> Needless to say, these autumns will be of the withered banana leaf and the
>   dried willow
> A thousand leagues of the world will tear me open
> From now on, who will regale my dear mother?[100]

The *kanshi* Shōen composed regularly and the diary she kept made up a crucial shared intellectual space for mother and daughter. This is most evident in Shōen's explanation of why she wrote in her diary daily. In an entry dated March 20, 1901, she writes:

> Sunny. In the previous notebook, I told myself that whatever happens today I would take up my brush. I have achieved forty continuous days because I thought of how difficult it would be to catch up later. When, after enduring sickness, I finally did reach this constancy, I rejoiced for myself, despite the fact that [the diary] brings no gain, and that if strangers see it after my death it will only invite mockery of my ignorance and lack of learning [*mugaku mushiki*].

But I think nothing of my name after death, only that the diary is a part of my daily routine and that it is easier to say things on paper than in person. I want it to be entertaining when I read it again at a later time, and [hope] that my mother will draw pleasure from reading it, since she looks forward to it the way some women wait for serialized newspaper fiction.[101]

Shōen was motivated by a number of impulses: to sustain a continuous record of her days despite her debilitating illness, to entertain her family members, and to serialize her life in the manner of newspaper novels. This desire to connect through writing and through interaction is evident in her notebooks from the early 1890s, when she was intent on viewing the most dramatic and controversial speeches in order to remain abreast of the latest events in Parliament, in spite of those who gazed judgmentally upon her. Even toward the end of her life, when her audience dwindled to a handful of readers, her desire to interact with the world around her persisted.

As Shōen's own life drew to an end in the seclusion of Ōiso, it was her relationship with her mother that inspired her to continue writing. Shōen's final poem, which was praised in the reviews of *Shōen nikki*, honors her mother as she faces death:

Gazing at Chinese peonies and tree peonies, I will go
With final words from my mother I leave
Traveling alone on a short trip over yonder, I am returning home[102]

Conclusion

Shōen's writings demonstrate the existence of educated and literate Meiji women who were offered new opportunities in an energetically transforming society but who also faced restrictions that limited their public roles. Shōen was drawn into public and national discourses in ways that shaped her understanding of herself as a Japanese woman. With her *kanbun* education, she was uniquely equipped to persist even after the end to the Freedom and People's Rights Movement and to adapt to a restrictive discursive order that prevented some of her early goals from coming to fruition.

Shōen's movement between the segregated worlds of governance and her household was also demonstrated by the shifts in her narrative voice in her diaries, the tone and stance of which adapted to her context. As an active observer and privileged interpreter of the public sphere, she was aware of the curious and invasive gazes that fell upon her. In her diaries she sometimes took on a third-person voice to give an authoritative analysis of her encounters. At home, she took charge as mistress of the household, asserting her demands and holding back none of her sharp observations. In her diaries, Shōen exposed a private self who was the obverse of her public persona; but both challenged the gender and discursive conventions of the Meiji era. In particular, the diaries reveal how literary communication was essential to Shōen's relationship with her mother, Taka, and with other women in her life. In sickness, reading and writing served as important bridges to her immediate as well as larger circle of writers and readers.

When Shōen's diary was published, her writing was interpreted, by virtue of its style, as lacking in femininity. In fact, the writing style of *Shōen nikki* did have an effect on its content *because* of how it was received by readers. Shōen engaged in politics and discourse in ways not readily available to other women. Shōen was both an object of discussion and a contributor to the shape of such discourses, first through her political speeches and then through her poetry, her trial, her essays, and her diaries. Her approach was indeed antithetical to the rising militarism presented by figures like Sohō. Despite the conventional "masculinity" and archaism of the *kanbun* mode, it helped Shōen give voice to her experience of confinement and exclusion. Her skill in *kanbun* and its derivations was foundational to her celebrity and success within the Freedom and People's Rights Movement and led to the publication and appreciation of her diaries after her death. Most important, these writings record the intense love of a mother who guided her daughter toward historical achievements through a *kanbun* education and a daughter's unwavering devotion and gratitude to the woman who was her most devoted reader. Fully in control of her style and expression, Shōen crafted a place for herself within a politically and culturally transforming society, and she helped provide other women with legitimacy and authority.

CHAPTER 3

SHIMODA UTAKO AND THE SCANDAL
OF THE EDUCATED FEMALE BODY

Introduction

In July 1907, *Osaka Asahi shimbun*, the second most popular newspaper of the period, with a readership of over 123,000, ran a profile of Shimoda Utako (1854–1936). Utako was the dean of Joshi Gakushūin, the women's division of the Peers' School (Gakushūin), where the Meiji aristocrats sent their daughters.[1] "If I were to make a list of women with authority [*erai fujin*] in our country based upon status, education, wit, judgment, and bearing, I would put Shimoda Utako first," wrote the profile's author.[2] Utako was a celebrity whose authority in society was tied to shaping women's education and to making women essential to a strong Japanese nation. As a woman working among powerful men, she was a target for scandal that grew out of both her social privilege and her gender.

The visual and conceptual contradiction evoked by a female public figure during the Meiji period is demonstrated by the scandal that erupted alongside the "*erai*" (esteemed) status that Utako's educational legacy had secured. Several months prior to this favorable profile, the socialist daily *Heimin shimbun* (Commoners' newspaper)—one of a number of socialist newspapers that were critical of the Meiji government—targeted Utako in a smear campaign from February 24 to April 13, 1907. It was carried out through a recurring column entitled *Yōfu Shimoda Utako* (Enchantress Shimoda Utako), which gave Utako a label that hinted at her power but also designated her as an otherworldly and mysterious femme fatale.[3]

Utako's life and career as an educator exhibited complex patterns of social relationships, political obligations, and public representations that shaped women's lives, especially within elite women's education. Utako was influential in the emergence of debate about women's intellectual potential. Understanding her role in Meiji women's education helps us grasp how various women's roles were defined against each other. That the femme fatale attack on Utako's character came from a socialist newspaper highlights the divide between privileged women and women of the laboring classes. The *Yōfu Shimoda Utako* column debuted just two days after Prime Minister Saionji Kinmochi (1849–1940) banned the Socialist Party on February 22, 1907. Reporters, especially those with socialist political views, were targets of government censorship. While *Heimin shimbun* ran the column for several months, it ended when the newspaper shuttered its doors due to pending legal actions to ban it.[4] The demise of the embattled socialist newspaper confirms Utako's social power.

There were several reasons why the *Yōfu Shimoda Utako* smear campaign, for which Utako was simply a convenient excuse, came about: the government suppression of all criticism, especially of socialist views in the post–Russo Japanese War years, and the outright commercialization of print media beginning in the early 1900s.[5] The existing cluster of socialist newspapers had declined in circulation since the buildup to the Russo-Japanese War in 1904. As nationalist fervor leading up to war with Russia strengthened, it drowned out the pacifist efforts of journalists like Kōtoku Shūsui (1871–1911) in the press. Following Japan's victory, the subsequent humiliation brought about by the Portsmouth Treaty opened the window for public criticism of the Meiji government. Amid this shift in momentum of nationalist fervor of popular support for war to discontent over the forfeiture of the victor's spoils, Prime Minister Saionji's comparatively liberal cabinet allowed a new Socialist Party to be revived in 1906. This allowed *Heimin shimbun* to be revived as a daily newspaper on January 5, 1907.[6] That the *Yōfu Shimoda Utako* column commenced shortly after Saionji banned the new Socialist Party suggests a number of things. First, Kōtoku Shūsui and his fellow journalists at *Heimin shimbun* were desperate to sell as many papers, and to do as much harm to the Meiji government, as quickly as possible. Second, Utako had enemies within the government who were willing to provide gossip to publicly humiliate her and who wanted to disrupt her relationship with the aristocracy, which was bolstered by her position at Joshi Gakushūin. Third, Utako was an important enough icon of Meiji women's education and national pride to be a worthy target for socialist journalists who sought to challenge the spread of nationalism and militarization.

By the 1900s, most of the Meiji press had already moved away from the principled and independent journalism of the 1880s' Freedom and People's Rights Movement. Growing circulation numbers indicated that a large number of newspaper readers were now seeking the sensational and salacious journalism that had once been relegated to articles on the third pages of newspapers (*sanmen kiji*) but was now front page and center of most popular newspapers.[7] *Yōfu Shimoda Utako* was such a column, and it both helped sell copies of *Heimin shimbun* and made a public impact for its socialist editors, despite its modest circulation. For its nearly month and a half duration, *Yōfu Shimoda Utako* appeared on a daily basis with private details of Utako's life, from her childhood, to her early career as an imperial court lady, to her alleged affairs with several members of the Meiji oligarchy. True to the genre, the column made sinister accusations, dredging up a ten-year-old scandal that accused Utako of aiding the first prime minister Itō Hirobumi's rape of a young aristocratic woman named Ujikita Kiwako.[8] By challenging Utako's integrity and legitimacy as an educator, the *Heimin shimbun* column perpetuated a connection between education and promiscuity that had already existed in popular discourses about women.

In our contemporary age of social media, a wide-reaching print media scandal like the one Utako experienced in 1907 could destroy someone in a public position of power. But what is true now was also true at the turn of the twentieth century: the professional damage a scandal could do was only as effective as the friends and colleagues it alienated. Utako's allies were powerful members of the Meiji elite, whereas her attackers were widely identified as radicals. While the indignity of the scandal was heightened by her friends' prestige, those friends also helped her weather the scandal. The July 1907 profile in *Osaka Asahi shimbun* is proof of Utako's powerful friends and the ability of a government-approved newspaper to cover up embarrassing and provocative stories of those with ties to the Meiji government as well as to the imperial family.

The negative publicity Utako got from *Yōfu Shimoda Utako* did not ultimately prevent her from leaving a respectable legacy. The Jissen Girls' School (Jissen Jogakkō), which she founded in 1899, is today Jissen Women's University (Jissen Joshi Daigaku), an institution featuring a four-year college, a two-year college, and secondary and primary schools, with over forty-five hundred female students matriculating each year. Even today, Utako is prominently featured in the university's promotional materials.[9]

During her lifetime, she authored over eighty monographs on Japanese women's education, manners, history, and literature. Her educational publications helped to shape Japanese women's identity through educational standards and the gendering of domestic management. These publications attest to the fact that Utako was a key proponent of the ideology of *ryōsai kenbo* (good wife, wise mother) in the late Meiji period, discussed in chapter 1, and that she supported a strict division of labor, designating the home as a woman's rightful and natural domain. Her legacy extends even to China: Chinese historian Joan Judge, who has written of the female Chinese students who studied abroad in Japan at Jissen Girls' School, describes Utako as the Japanese educator "most responsible for explicating and propagating [*ryōsai kenbo*] in the late Qing."[10] Utako's writings on education and femininity were imperially sanctioned, and she was rewarded with status and wealth, something that was rare for a Meiji woman.

Utako's role as a public figure raises interesting questions about the management of Meiji women's social respectability and influence when women's bodies and sexuality were also being actively debated as a matter of national concern. In an era when merely being photographed threatened to tarnish a woman's reputation, a woman who participated in a career or activity outside the boundaries of her home was vulnerable to objectification.[11] Male editors of literary magazines in the Meiji period commodified female writers by emphasizing these authors' appearances through prominent placement of their photographs, as Rebecca Copeland has written.[12] Jan Bardsley points to the role that a single photograph played in the expulsion of a female student from Joshi Gakushūin, whose picture had been submitted to a beauty contest without her knowledge.[13]

The tendency to commodify women continued into the Taishō period (1912–26), when women who sought to express themselves through writing, such as the Bluestockings (*Seitō*) coterie of the 1910s, were charged with "loose morals." The general sentiment was that women who appeared in public, whether in photographs or through their writing, were "asking" to be looked at with desire. Their very presence outdoors was an invitation to violation, a marker of availability. As Ayako Kano writes in her examination of the careers of Meiji actresses Matsui Sumako (1886–1919) and Kawakami Sadayakko (1871–1946), the onus was on actresses to "differentiate themselves from those women who engaged in sex work."[14] Even as women's bodies were being redefined as essential to the nation, there was an attendant anxiety over how to manage their potential sexual activity.

One element of Utako's work as an educator of girls was to continuously distance her students from associations with sex. The appearance of schoolgirls in public and the greater number of girls receiving an education raised alarms for some, who were fearful that women would be "damaged" or "led astray" by frivolous learning. Even though Utako's stated goal was to prepare girls to be "good wives and wise mothers," some objected to girls' venturing outside of the home to gain those skills. To achieve her goal and to justify the risks posed by education, Utako needed to embody an industrious, modern form of womanhood for twentieth-century Japan. Her vision for Japanese women still included the ideals emerging from a male-centered family system in which their life's mission would be to serve their fathers, husbands, and sons. But Utako also promoted these ideas within modern advances of the national education system and equipped girls within new opportunities as social citizens.

Shimoda Utako's Educational Foundations

To contextualize Utako's contributions to changes in women's lives, we must also consider those aspects of women's history that are not always associated with the modernization of women's status in the Meiji period. Utako was part of a particular strain of Meiji female educators who would appear out of place in an antiauthoritarian feminist history. As Margaret Mehl has argued, "Historians of the women's movement in Japan tend to equate the women's movement with opposition to the state and with Western liberal thought," and thus women's activities in the interest of the state are left unexamined.[15] For example, pioneers of women's education Miwada Masako (1843–1927) and Atomi Kakei (1840–1926) were educated in the Confucian tradition, supported the imperial state, and contributed to the modernization of women's education by advocating for it in public.[16] Utako is similar to Miwada and Atomi on all three fronts: she was highly educated and came from an intellectual family, she loyally served the imperial family, and she promoted education for the sake of the nation. She thus represents a side of the women's movement that is characterized by its connection to authority and support for the imperial government.

The scandals Utako would face were predicated on her privileged upbringing and her close ties to Meiji authority figures. To understand the nature of those scandals, we must first explore the foundations of her reputation. Born Hirao Seki in Mino Province, present-day Gifu Prefecture,

Utako hailed from a samurai family of scholars with nonconformist, anti-Tokugawa, proimperial political proclivities. Her maternal grandfather, Tōjō Kindai (or Nobuyasu, 1795–1878), was a well-known classical Chinese studies scholar (*kangakusha*). Her father, Hirao Jūzō, was a Confucian scholar (*jugakusha*), a specific area of scholarly specialization discussed in chapter 1.[17] As a descendent of scholars who studied Chinese texts on subjects related to statecraft, ethics, and language, Utako—like a number of her fellow female Meiji educators—studied canonical classical Chinese texts in addition to more typically feminine subjects such as *waka* (traditional Japanese poetry). Both of these educational foundations influenced Utako's writings, first in her support of a parliamentary monarchy and then in her desire to define a uniquely Japanese womanhood.

In 1871, Utako moved from Mino to Tokyo with her family. Within a year of arriving in Tokyo, she was recommended to serve as an attendant of the state (*goyō gakari*) of Empress Haruko. It was at court that she caught the attention of Itō Hirobumi, who is given special praise in Utako's official biography for his unwavering support of her career. He took an early interest in Utako's potential as a leader in women's education. Her appeal for both the empress and the Meiji oligarchy contributed to her later success in the arena of national girls' education.

Utako served for eight years as a court lady in the Meiji emperor's court, and in 1879, a month after leaving her post, she married Shimoda Takeo (d. 1884), a master swordsman, formerly of the Marukame domain in present-day Kagawa Prefecture in Shikoku. Though unparalleled in his swordsmanship, Takeo struggled to find employment in the post–Meiji Restoration bureaucratic system. He was already ill when he married Utako, and his health soon deteriorated to the point of immobility. To support her husband and herself, Utako opened the Tōyō gakkō (Tōyō School) for elite women, which she ran from their home from 1883 to 1885. Itō Hirobumi had enrolled his daughters in her school, where the daughters of two-time prime minister Yamagata Aritomo (1838–1922) and the first education minister, Mori Arinori (1847–89), also studied.[18] One of her students, Motono Hisako, later recalled that Utako cared attentively for the bedridden Takeo, who called out for her even during their lessons. After Takeo's death, Utako was reinstated to the court and given a post at the Kazoku Jogakkō (Peeresses' School), which was partly financed by the empress. Utako served as comptroller (*kanji*) and instructor in 1885 and then as dean (*gakkan*) from

1886 to 1906, when the Peeresses' School was incorporated into the Peers' School as its women's division.

The Meiji empress' support of Utako was a significant boost to the latter's prestige. In 1872 the empress gave her the name Utako (*uta*, lit., "poem") in recognition of her talents in *waka* composition. Utako embraced this honor and kept the name for the remainder of her life, reflecting her devotion to and endorsement by Empress Haruko.[19] It was likely a source of great pride that the empress' affection for Utako was based on her talent, for Utako was the daughter of only a midlevel "country samurai" (*inaka zamurai*), while most other court women were daughters of the aristocracy.[20] Her favored status was further confirmed in 1893, when she was entrusted with the instruction of the Meiji emperor's sixth and seventh daughters, the princesses Takeda Masako (1888–1940) and Kitashirakawa Fusako (1890–1974).

While women from families with political, intellectual, and financial resources and the willingness to educate their daughters had long had potential access to the highest levels of education, it was only in the Meiji period that expanding educational training for girls on a national scale became possible. It was in Utako's capacity as the princesses' instructor that she submitted an official request to travel to England and North America to observe the education of aristocratic and elite women.[21] During her trip she spent the bulk of her time in England, first in Brighton to study English and then in London. The wife of a Scottish minister of Parliament, Elizabeth Anna Gordon (1851–1925), who helped spearhead the Dulce Cor Library (also known as the Nichi-Ei Bunko, or Anglo-Japanese Library) in Tokyo, hosted Utako in London and arranged her school observations.[22]

During her time in England, Utako's mission shifted from studying the educational curriculum of the British royal daughters to examining the national educational system, which trained women of all classes. She extended her trip by an additional year in order to observe middle-class girls' schools. The historian Ozeki Keiko suggests that Utako may have been inspired by one of her hosts, Susannah Edwards, with whom she resided in a middle-class neighborhood in London.[23] Deeply impressed by Edwards's resourcefulness as a working mother, Utako observed that British women were able to work outside of the home to support their families rather than relying on a male breadwinner.

As she writes in her 1899 study of Western women (*Taisei fujo fūzoku*), her travels abroad awoke her to the need for the education of all Japanese women.[24] While studying English and learning about Western cultural and pedagogical practices—particularly with regard to girls and women—she observed that most British women were relatively educated and were, at the very least, literate—even those among the lower-middle class. As a result of these findings, she sent the following request to the empress in 1894:

> During my study abroad, I have witnessed how important women's education is, in particular for those below the middle class: the so-called "women of the masses" [taishū fujin]. I learned that their education could be a foundation for national prosperity [ryūkō]. Thus, I have carefully considered how critical this issue is for present-day Japan, and I would like, upon my return to Japan, to put my energies toward these areas of women's education.[25]

Her letter indicates that she was aware of her unique position to help implement change on a national scale for Japanese women as a whole. Such power had never been available to women before, and Utako appears confident that she can improve women's education more effectively than her male colleagues. She identified areas in modern society in which women might flourish, but these chosen fields were based squarely on a gendered division of labor. By enforcing this division, she held unprecedented authority over the lives of other women. Utako was granted an extension to her mission and returned home almost two years after her departure from Yokohama Bay.[26]

After returning home, Utako was not immediately released from her duties as dean of the Peeresses' School or as instructor to the princesses, but within a year of her return she founded the Teikoku Fujinkai (Imperial Women's Association). The association grew out of her close affiliation with the Meiji empress and helped to spread the notion of national duty among privileged women. Teikoku Fujinkai's mission was to advocate for the education of Japanese women of all classes. The founding documents of the group state that the association would honor (hōjiru) the empress as its president (sōsai) and that its main aim would be to "elevate the virtue, advance the knowledge, and strengthen the health of its members. Through collective support it [would] fulfill all the duties belonging to women."[27] As founder and chair of the Imperial Women's Association, Utako encouraged women to find employment and promoted education in order to train future female workers at every level of society. The association also sought to train women to be good housewives and manage a healthy home.

One example of an educational institution for lower-class women, established by Teikoku Fujinkai, was the sewing and maid-training school Shiritsu Joshi Kōgei Gakkō Fuzoku Kahi Yōseijo (Private Girls Industrial Arts School and Affiliated Maid Training School), which opened in Kōjimachi in 1899. In 1908, it was integrated into the Jissen Girls' Private School (Shiritsu Jissen Jogakkō) and Jissen Higher Specialized School (Joshi Kōgei Gakkō), with departments dedicated to home economics (*kaseika*) and practical arts (*gigeika*). The Higher Specialized School trained nutritionists, nurses, domestic assistants, and other women who pursued domestic professions. The charity school Jissen Jogakkō Fuzoku Jizen Jogakkō (Jissen Girls' School Affiliate Charity Girls' School), established in 1900, provided tuition, fees, and living expenses for girls whose families could not afford to educate their daughters.[28] It also provided instruction for maids whose employers allowed them time to gain literacy and other practical skills.[29]

The founding principles of both the Imperial Women's Association and the Jissen charity school included the need to shape the "influence" (*infuruensu* 感化) that women were to have on the world, particularly the influence they might have on their children and on the workforce of a new industrial society.[30] Utako saw this as a way to elevate women, to provide for their health, and to do so for the benefit of the nation. The curriculum at Jissen Girls' School was not entirely utilitarian, however. Those who could afford to study on the literature track received a rich education in Western and Eastern history, philosophy, literature, and mathematics. Seen through the lens of *ryōsai kenbo*, such instruction might seem merely part of a "finishing school" curriculum for future wives of the elite. But compared to a strictly utilitarian education, women's exposure to such an education meant that they were being offered a foundation for a rich intellectual life.

By the 1900s, Utako was one of the highest paid women of the Meiji period. When she was reinstated to the imperial court following her husband's death, she received an annual salary of one thousand yen.[31] This was an era in which a commoner family might get by on five to ten yen a month. Utako would go on to found and lead a number of other schools for girls: she was principal of the Meitoku Girls' School (Meitoku Jogakkō), established by the Ministry of Communication and Transportation, and founded the Patriotic Women's Evening School (Aikoku Fujinkai Yakan Gakkō), housed inside the facilities of the Patriotic Women's Society.[32] For these contributions to women's education in Japan, she received numerous honors, especially from the imperial household. In 1907, she was awarded the

Order of the Precious Crown (Fourth Class, Wisteria); in 1920, the mayor of Tokyo honored her for her service to the city; and in 1927, she was awarded the Third Order of the Sacred Treasure.

Utako's educational activities, which included bringing Chinese women to Japan to educate them at Jissen Girls' School, were part of Japan's colonial expansion into Asia. Her efforts reveal her belief in a state-centered educational system that supported a hegemonic social order. Educational historian Katayama Seiichi identifies Utako as one of a number of conservative educators of women in the Meiji 40s (1901–11) who saw *ryōsai kenbo* as the answer to women's "natural" employment as mothers and wives of healthy, strong citizens.[33] Utako's success in establishing numerous schools was due to her adherence to imperial and governmental aims to educate women for the sake of the Japanese empire; this is what made her, in some bureaucratic circles, the most highly esteemed of all Meiji women. Utako's patriotic efforts supported an imperial industrial framework that relied on women's wages and lifelong learning, as women's labor in the home and within industries would contribute to national wealth. While Utako's educational model offered new opportunities to women in Japan, it also maintained class, status, and national divisions.

A National Education for Women

Women's education in Japan emerged on a national scale as Meiji leaders planned a modern state-centered national education system. As mentioned in chapter 2, the Gakusei of 1872 was the first comprehensive legislation regarding national education. It built on one of the five articles of the 1868 Charter Oath of Five Articles, which stated, "Knowledge shall be sought throughout the world so as to strengthen the foundations of imperial rule."[34] The code affirmed the importance of educating women and men of all classes, and its implementation plan maintained that spirit. The concept of "wise mothers" (*kashikoi haha*), who properly disciplined their children, predates the Meiji period but reappeared after 1891 as part of the state-promoted slogan *ryōsai kenbo*.[35] This was due to the Imperial Rescript on Education (Kyōiku chokugo) of 1890, which outlined the Confucian virtues needed to shape women's identity and gender norms in the Meiji era. In the Imperial Rescript, the Ministry of Education expressed a need for an ethical foundation that they purported was lacking in the 1870s and 1880s as a result of overly Westernized education—a reference to missionary-founded schools that provided English language and religious instruction. As Carol Gluck has written, the Imperial Rescript "consisted of a Mito school beginning, which linked *kokutai* [national polity] with loyalty and filiality; a Confucian center, which enumerated the virtues that inform private and public human relationships, adding a modern injunction to civil disobedience and national sacrifice; and an imperial ending, which made the emperor the source of a morality that was said to be both indigenous and universal at the same time."[36] With this foundation, Japanese leaders sought to counter Western dominance in their region by creating their own universal morality upon which to build their own empire.

Numerous voices contributed to the discourse surrounding moral education in the early to mid-Meiji period: government bureaucrats, *minken* (popular rights) nationalists, court Confucianists, and Western-oriented philosophers all expressed strong opinions on how best to develop a successful national education system.[37] The fate of women's education had to be decided within this context, and numerous competing models emerged. Throughout the Meiji period, multiple intellectual and moral camps articulated their views on the proper instruction of women, with popular support shifting almost every decade from one camp to another. In the 1870s and early 1880s, the renowned Meiji Six Society (Meirokusha) believed that Japan should modernize according to Enlightenment ideology and Western ideals of individuality and social mobility, which would provide women with more rights.[38] Christian missionaries and educators ran Miss Kidder's School, the first private girls' school, as early as 1870. While some families saw a Westernized Christian education as a way to improve their daughters' marriage prospects, in the 1880s a backlash grew against English language and religious education, which was seen as promoting Westernization.

In the mid-Meiji period, advocates as diverse as Confucianists and socialists promoted further models of women's education. Confucianists attempted to revive Confucian moral practice among the populace as whole, with women in the main serving as the moral teachers for their children.[39] It is not surprising that this transitional cultural moment yielded competing positions on the education of women. Even Meiji educators were far from unified in the pedagogical approaches they promoted for the instruction of women. Ultimately, it was the Meiji government who held the authority to silence those models that were potentially critical of its rule, and Utako's enthusiastic support of the government's policies gave her a professional advantage over other educators of women.

As an agent of women's education in the Meiji period, Utako navigated her split allegiances and designed a system that would suit both the imperial bureaucracy and the oligarchs who sought to incorporate Western techniques. Utako saw the imperial court as the core of a uniquely Japanese identity, while the Westernization and industrialization promoted by the oligarchs would be essential for Japanese to compete internationally in a race that had started without them. It is evident that these allegiances gave her some freedom to execute her pedagogical vision within her schools.

For example, the women's *hakama* (kimono trousers) were popularized by Utako, when the Peeresses' School's *ebicha murasaki hakama*, the uniform of maroon trousers worn over a short kimono top, became synonymous with the schoolgirl. Historian of schoolgirl culture Honda Masuko has written that women's proper school attire had evolved from the early to mid-Meiji period, first from the male *hakama*, to the kimono with the obi sash, then to the Western dress with bustle, and finally to the female *hakama*.[40] Despite being a Meiji innovation, the female *hakama* was clearly more "traditional" than a Western gown but allowed students the mobility to participate in physical exercise. Utako, observing that robust girls would be better able to give birth to healthy children, promoted physical exercise as part of the curriculum for girls.

But Japanese society did not accept passively the ubiquitous presence of *hakama*-clad schoolgirls. While early in the Meiji popular imagination they represented purity and respectability, schoolgirls quickly became a target of moral alarm and then a source of entertainment with commercial value. As Melanie Czarnecki has argued, tales of *daraku jogakusei* (degenerate schoolgirls) came "to serve as cautionary markers while they simultaneously provided racy subject material."[41] Czarnecki further identifies Kosugi Tengai's (1865–1952) fictional work, *Makaze koikaze* (Demon winds, love winds), which was serialized in the *Yomiuri Newspaper* in 1903, as a turning point for the schoolgirl from being "ethereally sweet" to being susceptible to corruption.

In a series that ran in November 1902 in *Yomiuri shinbum* titled "Conversations with Leaders of Women's Education" (*Joshi kyōiku no shotaika no danwa*), Utako was one of the educators interviewed, specifically on the subject of "degenerate schoolgirls."[42] In the interview, Utako asserts that rumors of schoolgirls' degeneracy are "exaggerations" and insists that most of her students are quite docile. Finding that parents, particularly in rural areas, were becoming fearful of sending their daughters to Tokyo, she sought to reassure them that their daughters would be safe attending schools there.[43]

She may have been speaking in her own self-interest in 1902, for at the time when Utako was interviewed, the Peeresses' School, which she headed, was in need of more students. To be financially viable, the institution needed to recruit students from beyond the aristocratic classes, especially the daughters of wealthy commoners.[44] Fortunately for Utako and the Peeresses' School, the *hakama* was still a marker of privilege, aristocracy, and an indirect association with the Meiji empress herself, making it a uniform that privileged girls might aspire to wear.[45] While the methods of recruiting students and persuading reluctant rural parents were varied, Utako's argument for the benefits of girls' education was both practical and ideological. She was indeed challenging the moral panic over the schoolgirls' degeneracy, but she was also managing the financial solvency of an institution that could not survive on aristocratic patronage alone.

Domestic Science and Western Hygienic Practices

In her 1893 pioneering guide *Kaseigaku* (Study of household management), Shimoda Utako incorporated scientific knowledge into the instruction of everyday domestic practices. The knowledge included in *Kaseigaku* and similar manuals was not intended to train women as medical professionals but rather to enhance their skills as housewives so that they might be able to nurse their family members and keep them healthy. These practices included checking the pulse and body temperature; maintaining a hygienic sickbed environment; and assisting the medical doctors, who typically made house calls.[46] The management of hygiene and sanitized environments became the housewife's responsibility in the fight to quell contagious disease, and they were instructed to quarantine the sick from children and the elderly. In this way, domestic science and Western hygienic practices were repackaged as knowledge that would prepare a wife, mother, or daughter to safeguard her home and promote the health and strength of the nation. As Joan Judge's research and other research of modern women's education in East Asia show, domestic science education for women was a powerful modernizing force also in Chinese and Korean women's education and in those contexts helped to support the health and well-being of the emerging Japanese empire.[47]

Guidelines for home nursing (*katei kango*) were first included in the

Women's Higher Education Ordinance (Kōtō Jogakkō Rei) of 1899 and were then included in the Ministry of Education's instructor's manuals published in 1903.[48] The scientific nature of domestic healthcare enhanced the importance of a woman's role in the home and, by extension, their importance within society.[49] As national concern for citizens' hygiene and health expanded, ordinary women's practices gave rise to specialized practices.

While introducing new domestic responsibilities for the housewife, Utako also addressed the mental attitudes that would allow for the best execution of these tasks. In one textbook, Utako argued that a woman's commitment to hygiene management would contribute to her own mental health, as well as to public order.[50] The line between women's domestic and public duties was frequently blurred within the context of domestic science education. Because Utako's students engaged in social, nonfamilial, communal activities, they could more easily find employment outside the home upon graduation, if they so desired. An education in domestic science professionalized the modern housewife's role as a trained practitioner of domestic duties and found legitimacy and status for women within the family or the local community. By creating these specialized tasks for women through her articles and manuals, Utako asserted women's difference from men, as well as their societal importance in relation to men and to the nation as a whole.

In some of Utako's publications, such as *Kaji jisshūhō: Eisei keizai* (Practical guide to household chores: Hygiene and economy), she addresses practical skills like sewing, financial management, cooking, childcare, disaster response, home education, and care of the elderly and the sick. In other instructional texts, such as *Ryōsai to kenbo* (Good wives and wise mothers) and *Nihon no josei* (Women of Japan), she discusses more abstract topics, including the suitable ways to interact with one's husband or the new housewife's guide to etiquette (*reihō*).[51] Utako's publications reflected the influence of Confucian works, such as the classic *Onna daigaku* (Greater learning for women) attributed to Kaibara Ekiken (1630–1714), which was used to educate women, particularly of the samurai class during the Tokugawa era. *Onna daigaku* stated that women were to be obedient and respectful at all times and outlined a code of behavior specific to women. Utako drew her ideas from such sources but adapted her instruction to the needs of the era.

The code of behavior she adapted from various sources became useful when trying to criticize foreign practices. Her writings about her travels to

England reveal her disapproval of female scholars who "flaunted their knowledge in unbearably arrogant ways." She even writes, "The Japanese can learn nothing from this kind of educated Western woman," for such behavior was incompatible with the humility so cherished in Confucian ideals for women.[52] If she had to identify a Western model for Japanese women, Utako writes, she would have chosen someone like the suffragist Millicent Fawcett (1847–1949), who she describes as using her education to aid her husband's literary output. Though Fawcett was Western, her actions were in keeping with Utako's understanding of Confucian values. Utako concludes that women's education without the preservation of feminine virtues—which she understood to include elegance, grace, silence, and integrity—would be disastrous for Japanese women and the entire nation.[53] Utako tasked herself to limit Western women's cultural influence on Japanese women by touting the "true" characteristics of Japanese women, even as she served as one of the conduits of Western ideas.

Thus, when adopting Western educational practices she was careful to select those that were compatible with her ideals. In *Taisei fujo fūzoku* (Customs of Western women), Utako describes how literary study was part of the British curriculum: "For the English people, literature is not wholly about admiring a flower or the beauty of the moon. It is instead what is practical and profitable [*jitsuri jitsueki no mi wo musuberumono*]."[54] If the purpose of studying literary works for women had been to cultivate their aesthetic tastes, then this model of literary study was something that could have practical and profitable ends. This discovery was useful for Utako, who sought to make Japanese literary works, such as Murasaki Shikibu's *Genji monogatari* (*The Tale of Genji*), important resources for developing aesthetic sensibilities in her students. To prepare to defend Japanese traditional culture abroad, she packed volumes of *Genji monogatari* in her trunk for her voyage to England. In her writings, Utako contrasts the pragmatic literature of the West to the nonpragmatic nature of Japanese *bungaku*, what she refers to as *yūraku fūga* (refined play). This distinction allowed Utako to promote Japanese *bungaku* for women as both native and instructional. In her later years, she lectured regularly on *The Tale of Genji* for her students and published annotated guides.[55]

Utako's reverence for Japanese literature, and for *Genji monogatari* in particular, is evident in the introduction to *Shimoda Genji: shukan* (The tale of Genji lectures: First volume), where she recounts her youthful fascination with the author Murasaki Shikibu. As a child, she had been forbidden from reading *Genji monogatari,* so for years she had cultivated an intense desire to read the book. Her father advised against her reading the work: "Though *Genji monogatari* is a fine piece of writing [*meibun*], it is harmful to young girls and offers nothing beneficial to them [*eki naki sho dearu*]." He instructed her to "wait until after you have become an adult and have your own household."[56] Even so, she managed to peek at her aged monk instructor's copy of Kitamura Kigin's *Kogetsushō* (The moonlit lake commentary, 1673), which lay on his desk.

But not until Utako first arrived in Tokyo in 1871, when she consulted with local scholars who told her to first familiarize herself with *Genji monogatari* as an important foundation for literary scholarship, did her father assent to her reading the work itself. After her first full reading of *Genji monogatari* she admits to feelings of suspicion (*giwaku*) toward Shikibu and even "contempt" (*bujoku*) and revulsion (*ken'o*) at the passionate relations depicted therein. She attributes this early disappointment and resistance to her own "unnaturally" strict and rigid home environment (*hontondo fushizen ni genkaku de atta katei no kūkichū*).[57] But, she quickly adds that she recovered from this initial unease toward the work and discovered a new appreciation for its poetry, history, and culture. Her choice to study and teach *Genji monogatari* at Jissen Girls' School was in direct defiance of her father's pedagogical approach to women's education, and she charted her own path to its use as an educational text. She did not adopt the interpretation offered by her father but rather invented her own feminized reading of the work.

Her candid description of her girlhood revulsion toward a work that became a lifelong project provides an interesting angle with which to understand why she devoted her time to the teaching of *Genji monogatari.* In *Shimoda Genji shukan,* she points to some shared characteristics, that of gender and experience of court service, with the great Murasaki Shikibu. As a lady in waiting in Empress Haruko's court, she had also resided in a structure that was a replica of the imperial palace in Kyoto. Needless to say, it was a privilege few other *Genji* commentators could claim.[58] She turned to the study and teaching of *Genji monogatari* to rediscover what Heian women perceived to be their purpose or duty and how that might be incorporated into a history of Japanese women. Her intended readers were her *aideshi* (precious students or disciples), in whom she wished to instill the splendor of a *jun kokubungaku* (pure national literature), where they would learn of "true" Japanese femininity.[59]

The Old-Fashioned Woman and the New Woman

Not all ambitious, educated women shared Utako's vision of a national womanhood based in the wife's and mother's domestic duties—especially not those who sought independence from traditional familial obligations. The all-female literary coterie Seitō (Bluestockings) was a diverse group of writers, artists, poets, and journalists who drew inspiration from the eighteenth-century English women's salon. Utako and the women of Seitō were on opposite sides of a debate about what women could and should express through art and literature. But they faced similar forms of public persecution. The Seitō coterie began publishing an eponymous journal in 1911.[60] By then, Utako was a prominent educator seeking to produce women who would embody a traditional Japanese femininity, which, in the eyes of the Seitō women, simply reinforced women's inferior status and suffocated their creativity and independence.

The literary journal *Seitō* was envisioned as a platform for artistic, talented, and ambitious women who rejected their inferior status in Japanese society.[61] Hiratsuka Raichō (1886–1971), who was the first editor of the journal and one of the founding members, introduced the idea of the New Woman (*atarashii onna*) as an individual "advanced in thinking and frames of reference, one set upon questioning convention and the *ie* (family) system by which women are tied down."[62] In the popular media, however, New Women were often vilified for being "depraved and irresponsible." From Utako's perspective, women who prioritized their own artistic and intellectual development above allegiance to the family or the state ran counter to her Confucian-based values of placing the family unit first.

When *Seitō* set off a "journalistic boom" in articles on the New Woman, it gave rise to a new kind of criticism against modern, educated women.[63] The media focused less on issues of concern to the Bluestockings, such as artistic freedom, abortion, and economic independence, and more on the members' individual activities. As historian Jan Bardsley writes, although Bluestockings members were "acutely aware of how scandalous" their revealing and candid writings "would appear to the public, they nevertheless made explicit the connection between their private lives and public morality by writing frankly about their choices in their journal *Seitō*."[64] The group had its own internal disagreements, and the journal printed their debates over the definitions and consequences of women's limited choices and desire for financial independence and artistic freedom. One well-known discussion was sparked by Ikuta Hanayo's article in *Seitō*, "*Taberu koto to teisō to*" (On survival and chastity).[65] Hanayo had criticized the Japanese legal system for forcing women to choose between their chastity and economic survival, while others like Yasuda Satsuki objected by asserting that, for women, death was preferable to a loss of chastity. *Seitō* editor Hiratsuka Raichō weighed in by writing that she placed value on women's chastity, but not as a marker of their worth.

In her role as a prominent educator and advocate of women's education, Utako took it upon herself to counter *Seitō*'s New Woman with her own concept, that of the Old-Fashioned Woman (*furui onna*). Speaking with female journalist Isomura Haruko (1875–1918) for a series entitled "*Ima no onna*" (Women of today), Utako objected to Seitō women's efforts to redefine women's identity in Japanese society. Utako argued that while European women had jobs they could perform without the aid of men, Japanese women had yet to fully master even those professions conventionally deemed to be women's work. She stated that "the most urgent task is first to perfect the Old-Fashioned Woman, without even trying to aspire to the New Woman. For otherwise, this endeavor will definitely end in failure."[66] In her view, to achieve an ideal Japanese womanhood, women needed to master the skills traditionally assigned to them. She challenged women to overtake men in the professions specific to those skills and thus depicted Japanese women as existing in a state of unfulfilled potential. Utako considered this a pragmatic approach to defining the work that women should do. In her opinion the blame for not being treated equally lay with women who had failed to master the skills and knowledge most suited to them.

The term "old-fashioned woman" (*furui onna*) carries a multitude of negative connotations both in English and in Japanese. In the 1913 Japanese translation of Ellen Key's *The Morality of Woman*, the phrase "*furui onna*" was used as the Japanese equivalent of "conventional woman."[67] In that case, Utako's use of "*furui*" refers less to being outdated and more to a culmination of experience and wisdom—the idea of "tradition" in its most positive sense.[68] Utako's conventional Old-Fashioned Woman was traditional, Japanese, even Asian, but not Westernized, as she saw the New Woman. Her Old-Fashioned Woman drew from the accomplishments of educated and talented women of the past. In her view, only by emulating and surpassing these traditional role models would Japanese women of the Meiji period and beyond contribute to a strong Japanese nation. What distinguished this backward-looking model of womanhood from the models provided by her male counterparts, Utako believed, was the idea that women, given the opportunity and with the right amount of effort, could perform equally or perhaps better than men.

The differences in Utako's and the Seitō coterie's vision for Japanese women is seen starkly in *Seitō* editor Itō Noe's (1895–1923) open letter to Utako, published in October 1914. At the time, Itō stood at the helm of the journal, which had been struggling against censors and banned volumes. In her letter, she reveals that Utako submitted an article to *Seitō* with the explanation that it was "too inferior to publish" in more established journals and had therefore been submitted to Itō. Itō sought to expose Utako's condescending view of the coterie journal and to demonstrate that she had not been cowed by Utako's contempt. It is unclear whether Utako cared whether her article would be accepted for publication or that her accompanying letter was an end in itself—a message to the women of *Seitō* reminding them of their lesser place in society, as far as Utako was concerned. Itō confronts Utako's insult by pointing out the error of Utako's vision for women:

> In all the ways you have gone through life, you have been so clever that I cannot help but notice that there is some falsehood [*kyogi*] mixed in. Or you may be someone who is buried underneath a great falsehood. That is the feeling I have. The path that you have taken may in fact be an alternative path, a false path. Society's terrible misunderstanding of you may have something to do with that. I express my respect for your ability. I believe you have something quite extraordinary. But you have made a mistake in its use. If you had been able to see even a little of the wonder that is the truth, you would have been a much greater person. Or you would have taken a path that was not too different from our own. But there is the fact that convention wraps [you tightly] and has authority over you. Various circumstances restricted you. I deeply lament the fact that you entered that narrow and inflexible world of education.[69]

Here education is identified as producing and reinforcing conventions that bind most women, even as it is the medium through which women find a voice.

The antagonism of Utako by radical, less privileged women highlights the advantages Utako held in Meiji society due to her prominent position as a promoter of national women's education. The writer and socialist activist Kamichika Ichiko (1888–1981), who was also a member of Bluestockings, wrote a commentary on Utako in 1936, at the time of her death. In it, she stated that because Utako promoted *ryōsai kenbo* education, "the single most harmful ideology introduced for Japanese women in the modern era," she had damaged women's rights.[70] Kamichika refers to Utako's career-long affirmation of a patriarchal national order, a division of labor between men and women that kept women tied to the home, and a measure of women as only as important as their usefulness to their husbands and sons.

Kamichika identified government education officials as promoting "old-fashioned or conservative ideas." They in turn identified progressive activists like Kamichika "as dangers, and [treated] them as devils who disturb public morals." Kamichika states in her essay about Utako that "people with old-fashioned ideas are those who hold fossils in their arms and make useless efforts to warm them, hoping to bring them back to life."[71] This withering assessment leaves no doubt about where Utako stood in Kamichika's eyes, as opposed to women who sought social equality and political expression. To educated women who sought creative avenues for self-expression such as Kamichika and Itō Noe, the older, more experienced, and more privileged Utako reinforced the idea that educating women was a way to recruit them into society—but only under the condition that they use their education to fulfill exclusively feminine duties that were in service to the family or nation.

Despite the fact that Seitō writers and artists might not associate their work with that of late Meiji educators of women like Shimoda Utako, Hatoyama Haruko (1861–1938), or Tsuda Umeko, it is important to note that Kamichika and many of the members of the Bluestockings cohort were graduates of women's institutions of higher learning, namely, Japan Women's College (Nihon Joshi Daigaku) and Ochanomizu Girls' High School (Joshi Shihan Gakkō, Ochanomizu Daigaku). Many had participated in women's higher education as it had developed in the mid- to late Meiji period and were thus central participants in the Meiji redefinition of womanhood through education. *Seitō* editor Hiratsuka Raichō had once admired the work of her mentor, educator Naruse Jinzō (1858–1919), president and founder of Japan Women's University, with whom she had studied. But she was ultimately disappointed in his views on education, which excluded women from equal opportunities within society.[72] Like Utako, Naruse was only willing to go so far in granting women the intellectual freedoms afforded to men. Female writers and artists who sought to build identities outside the role of wife or mother saw the need to break from conventions of women's education system as they were promoted by the Meiji and Taishō governments. As the Swedish feminist writer Ellen Key wrote in 1911, "Conventional womanhood will ever have its strongest support in education," a sentiment that Utako embodied.[73]

In the struggle between the old and the new, the conventional and the radical, those closest to the government, namely, Utako, prevailed—including Utako. Itō's and Kamichika's frustration with Utako conveys generational and ideological differences that are couched in terms of *ryōsai kenbo*'s reinscription of a patriarchal family order. As historian Vera Mackie has stated, "It could almost be said that the official and the semi-official pronouncements on family and state," of which Utako was a key representative, "opened up a discursive space for the articulation of oppositional points of view on these matters."[74] The adversarial relationships between the Old-Fashioned Women and the New Women generated deep and active exchanges that helped to explain the narratives of womanhood emerging during the Meiji and Taishō periods and reflected the changing power dynamics within the discursive spaces that Utako sought to shape.

The Teacher as a Femme Fatale: The *Yōfu Shimoda Utako* Smear Campaign

Within Meiji discourse about women, girls' schools were routinely associated with an increased threat of sexual temptation, even when those schools, such as the Peeresses' School, were protected by imperial patronage. To legitimize the education of girls and women, it was necessary to adjust conventions, in practice as well as in language and imagery. Utako attempted this through her pedagogical essays, literary scholarship, and social commentary on women's manners and customs in order to define modern Japanese femininity and female national identity for an elite class of women. Conventions facilitate recognition, Judith Butler writes, and one's existence depends on one's recognizability, especially for marginalized members of society.[75] The conventions for girls and women that Utako promoted, for better or worse, helped to make Japanese women "recognizable" to a modernizing society. There were consequences for doing so, for "the terms that facilitate recognition are themselves conventional, the effects and instruments of a social ritual that decide, often through exclusion and violence, the linguistic conditions of survivable subjects."[76] The Meiji educational system, with its new set of conventions for Japanese girls and women, instituted a new order of survival, which favored a few over the many. Utako flourished because she embraced and expanded on these conventions, merging modern practices with her allegiance to the imperial family.

She shaped conventions by orchestrating perceptions through the production of a new discourse on women's education. This was most effectively executed by disassociating previous assumptions about the female body from the official language of education. Utako's efforts to speak for, and perhaps sanitize, the female body as an authority on domestic science and a mediator of knowledge from the West regarding modern women's education also promoted the presence of women in spaces of education, health care, and other areas where women had been previously absent.

What was revealed by the *Yōfu Shimoda Utako* smear campaign, discussed at the beginning of this chapter, is that she could not avoid exposing her own body to evaluation by the very language she popularized. Through the *Yōfu Shimoda Utako* newspaper series, Utako's body was co-opted by journalists who spoke of her in ways that undermined her intellectual output. The *Yōfu Shimoda Utako* column was a gendered campaign of sexual shaming. The series successfully marked Utako as a Meiji "enchantress" (*yōfu*) over the course of about forty days, offering snippets of Utako's allegedly libidinous private life and shameful past. Stories like "Utako Is Like a Prostitute," "Utako Falls in Love with Mishima," "The Defeat of an Adulterer," and "A Love Letter from Nanjō Fumio" accused Utako of conducting adulterous affairs; engaging in prostitution; and having romantic exchanges with multiple prominent scholars, politicians, and officials.

Most startling, perhaps, was the allegation that Utako was raped by the first prime minister, Itō Hirobumi.[77] The incident is described in the fifth installment, entitled "*Gōkan saretaru Utako*" (Utako was raped), claiming that when Utako was running Tōyō Girls' School and caring for her bedridden husband, she was invited to the mansion of Yamagata Aritomo, then a member of the House of Councilors. Leaving her sick husband at home, she set out for the posh Aoyama neighborhood. When she arrived, she was guided to an empty sitting room, whereupon a drunken Itō locked the door and, "like a lamb by a wolf, or a pigeon by a hawk," Utako, unable (or perhaps unwilling) to fight off her attacker, had "the flower of her chastity [*misao*] trampled upon [*hana no misao o jūrin serarenu*]."[78] Though the series mentions Utako's accomplishments, it repeatedly depicts her as a victim whose deviance was awakened by exposure to the sexual advances of, and even violation by, powerful men.

The series is attributed to journalist Fukao Shō (1880–1963) and was likely intended to not target Utako alone but also to slander her much more powerful allies: Meiji government officials and elites, especially Yamagata and Itō.[79] Professionally, *Yōfu Shimoda Utako* was a public relations disaster for Utako. At the time of its publication, she was competing with General Nogi Maresuke (1849–1912) to head the Peers' School, which in 1906 had incorporated the Peeresses' School, where Utako had served as president since 1895. Following the publication of *Yōfu Shimoda Utako*, Utako dropped her effort to head the Peers' School and resigned from her post. Her public humiliation was possible even though Utako was a widow and therefore the public had little reason to be concerned about her extramarital sexual activities, although the ideal would have been for her to remain faithful to her deceased husband.

The words stating that Utako was raped and each of the scandalous titles appearing on a daily basis served as proof that she was unfit to serve as an educator of women and as an advisor to the empress. If her status could be altered in the eyes of newspaper readers and ultimately the imperial court, *Heimin shimbun* would have succeeded in bringing about real consequences. The suggestion of *yōfu* behavior could taint the court and its leaders by association to Utako. The power at work within such slander is effective because of the ideal of womanhood as untarnished virtue that Utako herself helped to propagate. *Heimin shimbun* presented Utako as a woman who was sexually assaulted and consequently developed a voracious sexual appetite—in short, becoming a seductress. It accused her of masking her deviant behavior behind the facade of a successful educator and standard-bearer for Japanese women. The rape as depicted in *Yōfu Shimoda Utako* elicited its own form of punishment through the formation of public opinion of Utako's body. The allegation of being raped became the victim's own crime, with the implication that Utako, because she appears to have become a seductress, was ultimately at fault. In her study of the language used to describe sexual assault, the sociolinguist Susan Ehrlich emphasizes the politics of naming and articulating various forms of assault upon the female body and describes how feminist resistance to androcentric and sexist linguistic norms has included the "coining of new terms to express women's perceptions and experiences, phenomena previously unexpressed in a language encoding a male worldview."[80] In Utako's case, passages describing her alleged actions as published and circulated text altered the conditions under which she could carry out her duties as an educator of aristocratic women. By being called out as an enchantress or femme fatale, Utako could not avoid being seen as one. Thus we might call the litany of accusations speech acts that directly altered the legitimacy of her professional status. J. L. Austin describes such speech acts, arguing that the "issuing of the utterance is the performing of an action—it is not normally thought of as just saying something."[81] These attacks on Utako clung to her and threatened the image of refinement that she had cultivated over decades. Imperial advisors in particular were repelled by her damaged reputation as a contagion that might sully the imperial household and called for her resignation

The author of the series who was narrativizing Utako's private life was part of a broader political battle between supporters of the oligarchy and radical socialists.[82] Given Utako's alliances with members of the Meiji oligarchy and her intimacy with the imperial family, the *Yōfu* attack amounted to a political protest against hegemonic forces. *Heimin shimbun* was a provocative daily newspaper that appealed to a mass readership through politically charged content and sensational news. By attacking the legitimacy of those in power, journalists at *Heimin shimbun* sought to provoke popular unrest to bring about government reform. It was a staunchly radical newspaper most notably run by the socialist Kōtoku Shūsui, who was executed in 1911 for participating in the High Treason Incident, an alleged plot to assassinate the emperor, and Sakai Toshihiko (1871–1933), who openly voiced objections to Japanese imperialism and military activities in Asia.[83] *Heimin Shimbun* was frequently censored for criticizing the government, and the legal issues with the *Yōfu* articles about Utako led to the newspaper's eventual closing.[84]

While not political in a legislative sense, Utako's power was found in the discursive unity of the idea of "Japanese women," which she championed throughout her life. In other words, she had produced a new performativity of the female gender that was born in the Meiji period. Utako was equipped politically, financially, and intellectually to stave off a threat to her social status and authority after being described as a rape victim. This was in contrast with the media frenzy surrounding "degenerate schoolgirls" or "poison women" (*dokufu*): the targets of those attacks were more vulnerable members of society with restricted access to self-expression in print. Christine Marran has argued for the transgressive potential of the imagery of the "poison woman," a variation on the *yōfu*, used to describe a number of women who were charged with defrauding and poisoning their lovers. Marran describes how the poison woman served a "civilizing" role as a counterpart to the "good female reader," creating a binary that was "an implicit management of the female sex."[85] The character assassination of Utako focused specifically on her supposed promiscuity and replaced her image as a "good teacher" with that of the femme fatale. Her transformation was linked to the originating event of her alleged rape by Itō Hirobumi. The newspaper cited this alleged rape as a kind of original sin that both justified and damned all of Utako's suspicious activities thereafter.

Heimin shimbun's attack on Utako used her body as a surrogate for hegemony and, as Itō Noe's open letter to Utako mentioned earlier suggests, it was also an act of misogyny in the name of resistance to government authority and suppression that even women with views sympathetic to *Heimin shimbun* would recognize and lament. Utako's claim to authority opened up the kind of slander that would oust a powerful woman. The accusation of rape effectively made her unfit for service in the imperial court. This attack was made possible by the combination of her association with the imperial family and her work in women's education. Remarkably, Utako's survival is an example of Meiji female power, for the attack on her body and reputation failed to end her career.

Recreating Scandal through Fiction: The "Female Teacher" Utako

So much of the social discourse surrounding women in the public eye relies on gossip and scandal that the division between fiction and historical reality is blurred. Rather than seeking to separate the verifiable historical facts from the fictive narratives that shaped historical women's lives, it may be useful to engage the fictional narratives as a kind of historical experience. In Utako's case, the smear campaign and the trope of the enchantress cannot be untangled from the work she carried out in the public eye. The relationship between the trope of the enchantress and the work of the educator even appears in works of fiction that use Utako as a model. In 1903, the critic, journalist, and translator Uchida Roan (1868–1929) published a work of short fiction entitled "Josensei" (Female teacher), which offers an intriguing portrayal of a female educator of schoolgirls in the Meiji period.[86]

"Josensei" opens by describing the arrest of Yoshino Hanako, a young female student who was discovered at an inn with a young man and mistaken for a geisha, or "secret prostitute" (*jigoku*), and arrested by the police.[87] Under arrest, she told police her name and the name of her school, of which the protagonist Kasugano Shikako is the principal. The story follows the repercussions of Hanako's arrest and exposure, not only for Hanako but for everyone at her school. When Shikako learns of the young woman's arrest, she and her assistant discuss how to preserve the reputation of the school. While Shikako pities the doomed girl, her ambitions for her school and her fundraising efforts take precedence, and it is decided that Hanako will be publicly expelled from her institution.

By publicly shaming the girl, Shikako sought to prevent the incident from tarnishing the school's image, as well as her own, and the mass withdrawal of students by anxious parents. Shikako initially states that publicly humiliating Hanako would be "cruel" (*sorea zankokuda*) but eventually does so regardless.[88] Shikako herself inflicts the deadly blow upon Hanako, who is forced to stand on a stage during her sentencing:

> "I lament Miss Yoshino's talent. I regret her intellect. I had prayed for a talent like Miss Yoshino to enhance the honor of this school. Never did I dream that I would have to make such a sad announcement before you all. But rules cannot be broken. We cannot forgive one who has tarnished that most important thing to a woman: her chastity. Thus, in the name of this school, I expel this student, which amounts also to banishing her from society. Therefore, from this day on, the name of Yoshino Hanako will be removed from the registry of good ladies' names."
>
> And just as this solemn speech ended, Yoshino Hanako swayed and fell upon the stage with a cry and wept.[89]

Shikako's utterance renders Hanako a pariah in high society. The wording of the speech and its context within the school assembly render Hanako unchaste, stripping her of her good name.

Behind the scenes, Shikako must also deal with her own romantic affairs, which are suggested but not fully confirmed. In one scene following Hanako's arrest, a wealthy and powerful patron of the school, Count Yamato, sneaks in through a back door to visit Shikako in her office. Their tête-à-tête reveals something of Shikako's persuasive power and her strategic management of her school's image. When Shikako and Count Yamato speak, it is implied that they are lovers, that Yamato has promised to donate money to Shikako's school, and that yet another count (Izumi) has boasted of sleeping with her. Shikako promises to meet Yamato later at his home to discuss nonprofessional matters, and he suggestively expresses his fascination with "this serious madam principal [who] will transform into a completely different person."[90] During this conversation, Shikako's reactions surprise Yamato: she is insulted by his insinuations, at one point crying, much to Yamato's dismay. Shikako vigorously denies any relations with Count Izumi and only returns to her confident, beaming self when Yamato assures her that he will pay the rest of his promised donation and that he believes she has no other sexual relationships with her school's donors. The scene implies that Shikako is funding her school—and an impending trip abroad—by seducing donors, but she admits nothing directly. The tale presents Shikako, and the entire class of men and women who control Meiji high society, in a critical light as they exploit the blunders of a vulnerable girl and apparently exchange sexual favors for educational funding. The respectability of Shikako's name and body is also questioned in this tale, as her complicated personal life is revealed to readers.

In the tale, Roan shifts criticism from the schoolgirl to the parents and administrators, who enforce an arbitrary standard of sexual decorum based on economic and social status. The tale ends with a meeting between Shikako and a group of parents, during which she assures them of their daughters' safety and of the soundness of the school's reputation. Hanako's mother, the wife of a nouveau riche teahouse owner, then enters the meeting room to defend her daughter's honor, explaining that Hanako had been with her fiancé. She confronts Shikako as well, questioning her about the rumors of her affair with Count Izumi, which appear to be grounded in some truth given Shikako's conversation with Yamato in the prior scene. Even though Hanako's mother accuses Shikako and the other parents of hypocrisy, it is evident that Hanako's banishment from the school was not based on an intention to police sexual activity, for the scene reveals that the wives in the room were former entertainers of the demimonde who had married their wealthy patrons.

The story ends abruptly after this dramatic but fruitless confrontation: "Shikako departed on her journey to observe girls' education abroad. Many newspapers praised the lady's bravery and celebrated her efforts to further women's education."[91] Shikako's durability in the tale can be read as a result of self-preservation, but it also reveals the injustice of social practices that protect the wealthy and powerful. Shikako merely played along with the rules of society, all the while aware that they arbitrarily punished those who did not have the backing or planning to protect themselves.

Roan drew from historical events in his fiction to portray the hypocrisy of those government officials promoting traditional feminine virtue. Literary scholar Yi Sunshin has pointed out that scholars of Uchida Roan originally overlooked analysis of "Josensei," believing it to be written by Guy de Maupassant due to its inclusion in a collection of Roan's translations of

Maupassant's short fiction.[92] But no comparable original for "Josensei" has been found among Maupassant's works, and the plot clearly reflects a historical event in Japan, with characters who closely resemble Japanese historical figures. Roan was likely inspired by a work of "degenerate schoolgirl" fiction: Kosugi Tengai's *Makaze koikaze*, mentioned earlier, which appeared in *Yomiuri shimbun* a month prior to the publication of "Josensei."[93]

While "Josensei" is not one of Roan's best-known forays into fiction writing, it provides additional insight into perceptions of private women's education and the place of women in late Meiji society. In a 1913 special volume on women's issues published by the monthly literary magazine *Chūō Kōron*, Roan reveals his support for the women of Seitō and his desire for even more independence for women:

> We cannot escape the fact that women's self-awareness in Japan is still weak. It is a movement like those bestowed on women by men, and not one that emerged from women's own inner voices [*innā boisu*]. Needless to say, most women will not connect with the breed of New Women, and among these New Women there are only a few who would truly sacrifice themselves for this as an issue vital to themselves and to their fellow women. But it is not empty like the women's issues proclaimed by men [*otoko kara tonaerareta fujin mondai*] up until now.[94]

Roan held a progressive view of a "true" women's movement that came from women and demanded more freedom and equal status in their relations with men, something similar to what Seitō achieved in the 1910s.

Roan's story draws attention to the hypocrisy of high society as it seeks to scapegoat a young girl to sustain the image of ideal virtue associated with aristocratic women. What is intriguing about this story in relationship to *Yōfu Shimoda Utako* is Roan's suggestion that Shikako, modeled after Utako, held the power herself to utter the words used to transform and ruin Hanako's life. Her words level a physical blow upon Hanako, who "swayed and fell upon the stage with a cry and wept."

Conclusion

The *Yōfu Shimoda Utako* newspaper columns that threatened Shimoda Utako's career in 1907 represent a moment when two sides of a powerful woman's reputation competed for attention, one side reflecting the work of her mind and the other reflecting the imagined acts of her body. Utako was no passive victim of the media: she was a prolific writer with numerous publications and with well-publicized service to and highly regarded by the imperial family. Her successful educational endeavors made her a target for criticism and vicious rumors but also allowed her to ultimately survive. The discourse of women's education empowered and, at the same time, humiliated women. It also reveals deep entanglements created by hierarchies of access to financial support, government authorization, and social standing that were symptomatic of the gendered power at work in Utako's execution of Meiji women's education. Jissen Jogakkō and Utako's legacy have survived for over a century. Utako's contributions to the early Japanese women's movement had contradictory effects and made scapegoats of those who were not in lockstep with her ideals. Yet she too was in a position to overcome discourses embedded into women's power and education. We recognize in her the contradictory forces pushing and pulling the women who participated in and sought meaning in the educational endeavor.

CONCLUSION

The previous chapters examined the contradictory forms of intellectual and cultural capital that powerful Meiji women drew upon to wield influence in the areas of education and gendered conventions in the Meiji public and private spheres. Represented most prominently by Empress Haruko, elite, educated women helped to produce discourses that supported their agency in ways that do not fit easily into a feminist history of the early twentieth century. The empress herself, who was groomed from childhood to marry and serve the emperor in his court, was given an entirely modern set of responsibilities that redefined what a Japanese empress could do. She was essential to the modern imperial nation-state and made herself indispensible. Service to the Meiji empress functioned quite differently for Nakajima Shōen and Shimoda Utako. Shōen refers to her court service as a starting point from which she stepped out into the Freedom and People's Rights Movement, whereas Utako became the empress' deputy in the field of elite women's education. For her loyal service, Utako received generous financial support and bureaucratic authority, making her one of the most powerful Japanese women of the early Meiji period. Educators like Utako, and even Shōen, who taught women *kanbun* in her home, shaped women's work and identity by creating new connections between women's domestic and social skills and their importance to society and the nation as a whole. These connections and communities of women were shaped within cultural and professional institutions that were made possible by the modernization of Japanese society, but they were accessible only to women of privileged strata, thereby excluding most women from its monetary and cultural advantages.

These three women worked in the service of the nation-state, but a narrative that relegates them to supporting and subordinate roles fails to recognize that these women were forging new practices and conventions in Meiji society and creating foundations upon which a more independent and equal vision of womanhood could be imagined. In fact, we might say that despite the women's discourses these Meiji women adhered to in their writings, in practice, they were already pushing the boundaries of permissible behavior for Japanese women, and doing so under the guise of modernization.

These women are an important point of comparison and resistance for women of Seitō, who resisted patriarchy and struggled against "older sisters" and "predecessors" who cultivated the very conventions that restricted them in Meiji society. The hierarchies established in the mid-Meiji period among women carry their own significance. What Haruko, Utako, and Shōen were doing did not merely replicate the patriarchal enforcement of female norms. In fact, the women-centered relationships they formed continue to be duplicated in modern society.

Powerful Meiji women had identities that were unique to them, that did not fit into convention—they were extraordinary and also necessary to the production of normative standards. Shōen, the exceptional *kanshi* poet and *kanbun* scholar; Utako, the exceptional educator; and Haruko, the exceptional monarch, all challenged in practice the familiar norm of "mothers" of modern women.

The narrative of women's empowerment must include a consideration of women's power as being able to subjugate others, especially other women. Feminist histories, by identifying empowerment more as a power to accomplish something rather than as a power over others, raise the question of whether women's power over others is in fact the desired goal of some women's empowerment. That some women achieve power equated with men is not enough to benefit women's status overall. Each execution of power must reflect awareness of the various women who are disproportionately influenced by those at the top.

These powerful Meiji women were subject to misogynistic attacks, and yet they used public platforms to endorse new and at times restrictive conditions for women. But they did so while enjoying exceptions on the basis of their prominence. The ways they managed and executed that power can provide important lessons for further exploration of women's power.

GLOSSARY

Aoyama Chise	青山千世
Aoyama Enkō	青山延光
Arisugawanomiya Taruhito	有栖川宮熾仁
atarashii onna	新しい女
bakufu	幕府
Bān Zhāo	曹大家
Bankoku kōhō	万国公法
bōyomi	棒読
Chūgaku kanbun tokuhon	中学漢文読本
daimyō	大名
danshaku	男爵
daraku jogakusei	堕落女学生
Ding Wei Liang	丁韙良
dokufu	毒婦
eki naki sho dearu	益無き書である
Ema Saikō	江馬細香
erai fujin	偉い婦人
Fuei shinsetsu	婦嬰新説
fujinkai no kifujin	婦人界の貴婦人
Fujo kagami	婦女鑑
Fukao Shō	深尾韶
Fukuzawa Yukichi	福沢諭吉
furui onna	古い女
gakkan	学監
Gakusei	学制
Gakushūin	学習院
Gamō Shigeaki	蒲生重明

genbun itchi	言文一致
genjitsu no Shina	現実のシナ
Genrōin	元老院
gogon zekku	五言絶句
gōjū	剛柔
"Gōkan saretaru Utako"	強姦されたる歌子
goyō gakari	御用係
gyōkei	行啓
Hatoyama Haruko	鳩山春子
Heimin shimbun	平民新聞
Hiratsuka Raichō	平塚らいてう
Ichijō Masako	一条美子
ikita mohan	生きた模範
inaka zamurai	田舎侍
Inoue Hisashi	井上ひさし
Itagaki Taisuke	板垣退助
Itō Hirobumi	伊藤博文
Itō Noe	伊藤野枝
jigoku	隠売婦
jihō	侍補
Jinbutsu gaden	人物画伝
Jiyū Minken Undō	自由民権運動
jokan	女官
jokōba	女紅場
joryū gaka	女流画家
"Josensei"	女先生
Joshi kanbun tokuhon dai 4-hen	女子漢文読本 第 4 編
Joshi kokubun tokuhon	女子漢文国分読本
"Joshi o shite sho o yomashimu bekarazaru ron"	不可使女子讀書論
jugakusha	儒学者
Kaibara Ekiken	貝原益軒
kaikaku	改革
Kakubutsu nyūmon	格物入門
Kamichika Ichiko	神近市子
kanbun	漢文
kanbun kundokutai	漢文訓読体
kanbun kyōjuhō	漢文教授法
kanbunchō	漢文調
kanbunmyaku	漢文脈

kangakusha	漢学者
kanji kanamajiri	漢字仮名交じり
kanri bujoku zai	管理侮辱罪
kanshi	漢詩
Kasugano Shikako	春日野鹿子
Katō Shihō [Hyōko]	加藤紫芳 (瓢乎)
kazokurei	華族令
"Kenpu nanigashi den"	賢婦某伝
Kinnō tōbaku	勤皇倒幕
Kinsei ijin den	金星偉人伝
kōgō	皇后
Kokubu Misako	国分美佐子
kokugo oyobi kanbun ka	国語及漢文科
Kokumin no tomo	国民之友
kokuminka	国民化
kōkyū	後宮
Kosugi Tengai	小杉天外
kōtai	後退
kuge	公家
Kyōgaku seishi	教学聖旨
Makaze koikaze	魔風恋風
masurao buri	益荒男ぶり
meibun	名文
Meiji kōsetsuroku	明治孝節録
Meiji tennō ki	明治天皇記
Meirokusha	明六社
Miura Kanō	三浦叶
Miwada Masako	三輪田雅子
Mori Ōgai	森鴎外
Mōshi	孟子
Motoda Nagazane	元田永孚
Nakajima Shōen	中島湘煙
Nakamura Ritsuen	中村栗園
nikubuto	肉太
oboshimeshi	思し召
Ōiso	大磯
Onna daigaku	女大学
Onna nidai no ki	女二代の記
Onna shisho	女四書

Osaka Asahi shimbun	大阪新聞
Rikken Seitō	立憲政党
riseiteki na seikatsu taido	理性的な生活態度
Risshisha	立志社
ryōsai kenbo	良妻賢母
Ryū Kyō	劉向
Sabishiki miyai	寂しき宮居
sadaijin	左大臣
seiryōden	清涼殿
Seiyō jijō	西洋事情
senkyōshi	宣教使
Senmon gakumu kyoku	専門学務局
shichigon risshi	七言律詩
Shimoda Utako	下田歌子
Shina shigaku	シナ史学
shindō	神童
Shiritsu Joshi Kōgei Gakkō Fuzoku Kahi Yōseijo	私立女子工芸学校付属婢養成所
shizoku	士族
Shōen nikki	湘煙日記
Shōgaku hitsudoku Onna sanjikyō	小学必読女三字経
Shōken kōtaigō	昭憲皇太后
shūkai jōrei ihan	集会条例違反
Sōma Kokkō	相馬黒光
"*Sonnō jōi*"	尊王攘夷
Tanahashi Ayako	棚橋綾子
taoyame buri	手弱女ぶり
Teikoku kyōikukai	帝国教育会
tenkai	転回
Tōjō Kindai	東条琴台(信耕)
Tōyō gakkō	桃夭学校
tōyōgaku	東洋学
Tōyō Kaiga Kyōshinkai	東洋絵画共進会
"Tsuge Shirōzaemon"	津下四郎左衛門
Uchida Roan	内田魯庵
Utsunomiya Takako	宇都宮多歌子
Wage onna shishō	和解女四書
Wakae Nioko	若江薫子
Wen xuan	文選

Yajima Kajiko	矢島楫子
yakudoku	訳読
"Yamaguchi Shigenobu den"	山口重信伝
Yamakawa Kikue	山川菊栄
Yamakawa Michiko	山川みち子
Yamawaki Fusako	山脇房子
Yanagiwara Naruko	柳原愛子
yōbutsu	妖物
yōfu	妖婦
Yokoi Heihachirō	横井平八郎
Yoshino Hanako	吉野花子
yūraku fūga	遊楽風雅

NOTES

Introduction

1. Bernie Silberman, "The Bureaucratic State in Japan: The Problem of Authority and Legitimacy," in *Conflict in Modern Japanese History: The Neglected Tradition,* ed. Tetsuo Najita and J. Victor Koschmann (Princeton, NJ: Princeton University Press, 1982), 237.

2. Women made up 80 percent to 90 percent of textile industrial workers from the 1900s to 1920s. Elyssa Faison, *Managing Women: Disciplining Labor in Modern Japan* (Berkeley: University of California Press, 2007), 8–9; E. Patricia Tsurumi, *Factory Girls: Women in the Thread Mills of Meiji Japan* (Princeton, NJ: Princeton University Press, 1990), 10.

3. Shizuko Koyama, *Ryosai Kenbo: The Educational Ideal of "Good Wife, Wise Mother" in Modern Japan,* trans. Stephen Filler (Leiden, Netherlands: Brill, 2015).

4. Nakamura Masanao used the term in the journal *Meiroku zasshi* (1874–75) in an introduction to John Stuart Mill's *On Liberty* (1859). The first use of *ryōsai kenbo* in its national ideological sense was in the journal *Jokan,* beginning with the first issue in August 1891. Koyama, *Ryōsai Kenbo,* 4. Fukaya Masashi, *Ryōsai kenbo shugi no kyōiku* [Education of ryōsi kenbo ideology], Kyōiku meicho sensu (Tokyo: Reimei Shobō, 1998), 156.

5. Takashi Fujitani, *Splendid Monarchy: Power and Pageantry in Modern Japan* (Berkeley: University of California Press, 1998), 4. Fujitani cites Benedict Anderson's description of the paradox that "the objective modernity of the nations to the historian's eye" exists alongside "their subjective antiquity in the eyes of nationalists."

6. Henri Lefebvre, *The Production of Space,* trans. Donald Nicholson-Smith (Cambridge, MA: Wiley-Blackwell, 1992), 33.

7. Wakakuwa Midori, *Kōgo no shōzō: Shōken Kotaigō no hyōshō to josei no kokuminka* [Portrait of the empress: Representations of the dowager empress Shōken and the nationalization of women] (Tokyo: Chikuma Shobo, 2001). All translations are my own unless otherwise indicated.

8. Marnie S. Anderson, *A Place in Public: Women's Rights in Meiji Japan* (Cambridge, MA: Harvard University Asia Center, 2010); Mara Patessio, *Women and Public Life in Early Meiji Japan: The Development of the Feminist Movement* (Ann Arbor: Center for Japanese Studies, University of Michigan, 2011); Elizabeth Dorn Lublin, *Reforming Japan: The Woman's Christian Temperance Union in the Meiji Period* (Vancouver, BC: University of British Columbia Press, 2010).

9. In fact, the revised newspaper law (*kaisei shinbunshi jōrei*) of 1883 made it illegal for women to be editors, publishers, or printers of newspapers. Ōki Motoko, *Jiyū minken undō to josei* [The Freedom and People's Rights Movement and women] (Tokyo: Domesu Shuppan, 2003), 38.

10. Hirata Yumi, *Josei hyōgen no Meijishi: Higuchi Ichiyo izen* [Women's expression as Meiji history: Before Higuchi Ichiyō] (Tokyo: Iwanami Shoten, 1999), 12.

11. Rebecca L. Copeland, *Lost Leaves: Women Writers of Meiji Japan* (Honolulu: University of Hawai'i Press, 2000), 89.

12. Anderson, *A Place in Public.*

13. Lublin, *Reforming Japan.*

14. Christine L. Marran, *Poison Woman: Figuring Female Transgression in Modern Japanese Culture* (Minneapolis: University of Minnesota Press, 2007).

15. For further discussion, see Takada Chinami, Nakagawa Shigemi, and Nakayama Kazuko, eds., *Josei sakkashū, Shin Nihon koten bungaku taikei, Meiji hen v.23.* (Tokyo: Iwanami Shoten, 2002), 521–36.

Chapter 1

1. Kyōikushi Hensankai, *Meiji ikō kyōiku seido hattatsushi* [History of the development of the educational system since the Meiji period] (Tokyo: Kyōiku Shiryō Chōsakai, 1964–65), 288–89. Of the twenty-eight hours each week, five to six would be set aside for *kokugo* (national language studies), and another six to seven would be devoted to a combination of history/geography (*rekishi/chiri*), mathematics (*sūgaku*), and science (*rika*). Male students attending public middle schools would study six to seven more hours of *Kokugo oyobi kanbun* a week during every year of middle school.

2. Sharon H. Nolte and Sally Ann Hastings, "The Meiji State's Policy Toward Women, 1890–1910," in *Recreating Japanese Women, 1600–1945*, ed. Gail Lee Bernstein (Berkeley: University of California Press, 1991), 151–74; Margaret Mehl, "Women Educators and the Confucian Tradition in Meiji Japan (1868–1912): Miwada Masako and Atomi Kakei," *Women's History Review* 10, no. 4 (2001): 579–602; Sally A. Hastings, "Hatoyama Haruko: Ambitious Woman," in *The Human Tradition in Modern Japan*, ed. Anne Walthall (Wilmington, DE: SR Books, 2002), 81–98; Umeko Tsuda and Yoshiko Furuki, *The Attic Letters: Ume Tsuda's Correspondence to Her American Mother* (New York: Weatherhill, 1991); Martha C. Tocco, "Norms and Texts for Women's Education in Tokugawa Japan," in *Women and Confucian Cultures in Premodern China, Korea, and*

Japan, ed. Dorothy Ko, JaHyun Kim Haboush, and Joan R. Piggott (Berkeley: University of California Press, 2003), 193–218.

3. Saitō Mareshi, *Kanbunmyaku to kindai nihon: mō hitotsu no kotoba no sekai*, NHK Books 1077 (Tokyo: Nihon Hōsō Shuppankai, 2007), 130.

4. Joshua A. Fogel, "Kano Naoki's Relationship to Kangaku," in *New Directions in the Study of Meiji Japan*, ed. Adam L. Kern and Helen Hardacre (Leiden, Netherlands: Brill, 1997), 358.

5. Katano Masako, "Kindai kōgōzō no keisei" [The construction of the image of the modern empress], in *Kindai Tennōsei no keisei to Kirisutokyō* [The construction of modern imperial ideology and Christianity] (Tokyo: Shinkyō shuppansha, 1996), 112.

6. Benjamin Duke, *The History of Modern Japanese Education: Constructing the National School System, 1872–1890* (New Brunswick, NJ: Rutgers University Press, 2009), 268.

7. The Imperial Will on Education is distinct from Inoue Kowashi's Imperial Rescript on Education (Kyōiku chokugo) of 1890. Inoue's version includes the modern western principles of nationhood (*kokutai*) in the "Rescript," based on the German model. Duke, *The History of Modern Japanese Education*, 361.

8. Duke, *The History of Modern Japanese Education*, 262.

9. Miura Kanō, *Meiji no kangaku* [Chinese studies of the Meiji period] (Tokyo: Kyūko shoin, 1998), 403–4.

10. Miura Kanō, *Meiji no kangaku*, 18.

11. Miura Kanō, *Meiji no kangaku*, 23.

12. Miura Kanō, *Meiji no kangaku*, 405.

13. Miura Kanō, *Meiji no kangaku*, 405.

14. The exception is Sally Hastings's incisive analysis of her role in the implementation of Western clothing in the imperial court. Sally A. Hastings, "The Empress' New Clothes and Japanese Women, 1868–1912," *Historian* 55, no. 4 (1993): 677–92.

15. Kunaicho, Japan, and Meiji Jingu (Tokyo, Japan), *Shōken Kōtaigo jitsuroku* (Tokyo-to Bunkyo-ku: Yoshikawa Kobunkan, 2014). Kunaicho, Japan, *Meiji Tenno ki* (Tokyo: Yoshikawa Kobunkan, 1968).

16. Donald Keene, *Emperor of Japan: Meiji and His World, 1852–1912* (New York: Columbia University Press, 2002), 105.

17. Joshua S. Mostow, "Modern Constructions of *Tales of Ise*: Gender and Courtliness," in *Inventing the Classics: Modernity, National Identity, and Japanese Literature*, ed. Haruo Shirane and Tomi Suzuki (Stanford, CA: Stanford University Press, 2000), 96–119.

18. Takie Sugiyama Lebra, *Above the Clouds: Status Culture of the Modern Japanese Nobility* (Berkeley: University of California Press, 1995), 43.

19. Lebra, *Above the Clouds*, 28.

20. Katano Masako, *Kōgō no kindai* [The empress's modernity] (Tokyo: Kodansha, 2003), 24–25. Meiji Jingū, *Shōken Kōtaigō jitsuroku*, 1: 66–67.

21. As a *jokan* of *kuge* background, Yamakawa Michiko was stationed in closer prox-

imity than lower-ranking women who had worked there for longer. Yamakawa Michiko, *Jokan* (Tokyo: Jitsugyō no Nihonsha, 1960).

22. Lebra, *Above the Clouds*, 30.

23. Yamakawa Michiko, *Jokan*, 77–79.

24. Yamakawa Kikue, *Onna nidai no ki: Watashi no han jijoden* (Tokyo: Nihon Hyōron Shinsha, 1956), 50.

25. Katano Masako, *Kōgō no kindai*, 123.

26. Hastings, "The Empress' New Clothes," 682; Keene, *Emperor of Japan*, 404.

27. *Shōken Kōtaigō jitsuroku*, 1: 480–81. Von Mohl had served as cabinet secretary to Augusta of Saxe-Weimar-Eisenach, the queen of Prussia and the first empress of Germany. He and his wife Wanda, the Countess von der Groeben, served the Imperial Household Ministry (Kunaishō) as advisors from 1887 to 1889, during which time they informed the empress of Western court conventions. Ottmar von Mohl, *Doitsu kizoku no Meiji kyūtei ki*, trans. Kanamori Shigenari (Tokyo: Shinjinbutsuōraisha, 1988), 54. Katarzyna J. Cwiertka, *Modern Japanese Cuisine: Food, Power, and National Identity* (London: Reaktion Books, 2012), 18.

28. Duke, *The History of Modern Japanese Education*, 257–80; Keene, *Emperor of Japan*, 328–29; Wakakuwa, *Kōgo no shōzō*, 200–208.

29. Hastings, "The Empress' New Clothes," 683.

30. Katano, "Kindai kōgōzō no keisei," 112. Meiji Jingū, *Shōken Kōtaigō jitsuroku*, 1:332.

31. Keene, *Emperor of Japan*, 172.

32. Keene, *Emperor of Japan*, 525.

33. Keene, *Emperor of Japan*, 525.

34. Katano, *Kōgō no kindai*, 25–26.

35. Yamakawa Kikue, *Onna nidai no ki*, 50. Socialist feminist writer Yamakawa Kikue wrote a biography of her mother, Aoyama Chise, who was a highly educated member of a family of scholars from the Mito domain. The text reveals that Aoyama was respected and sought after as a tutor and educator for elite women.

36. Katano, "Kindai kōgōzō no keisei," 96.

37. Katano, "Kindai kōgōzō no keisei," 96.

38. Yamakawa Michiko, *Jokan*, 57.

39. Wakakuwa, *Kōgō no shōzō*, 334.

40. Wakakuwa, *Kōgō no shōzō*, 334.

41. Wakakuwa, *Kōgō no shōzō*, 334.

42. Utsunomiya Takako, ed., *Joshi kanbun tokuhon dai 4-hen* (Tokyo: Keigyōsha, 1899).

43. Akiyama Shirō, ed., *Chūgaku kanbun tokuhon* (Tokyo: Kinkōdō, 1894).

44. Nakamura Kazu [Ritsuen], "Joshi o shite sho o yomashimu bekarazaru ron," in Akiyama Shirō, *Chūgaku kanbun tokuhon*, 33–35. The scholar Ritsuen was a contemporary of Fukuzawa Yukichi's father, and Fukuzawa's autobiography tells of how Ritsuen had begun to give "special attention to Sun-tzu in his lectures and he had even orna-

mented the entrance to his house with ancient armor." Fukuzawa mentions avoiding visits to Ritsuen's school in order not to run into "young pupils of fiery spirit," who had strong antiforeign sentiments. Fukuzawa Yukichi, *The Autobiography of Fukuzawa Yukichi*, trans. Eiichi Kiyooka (New York: Columbia University, 2007), 230.

45. Nakamura, "Joshi," 34.

46. No other textbook is attributed to Utsunomiya Takako, but as editor of *Joshi kanbun tokuhon dai 4-hen*, she would have been proficient in *kanbun*.

47. Miura, *Meiji no kangaku*, 428–29. *Kakubutsu nyūmon* is attributed to Ding Wei Liang, William Alexander Parsons Martin's name rendered in Chinese.

48. Kondō Yoshiki, ed., *Meiji kōsetsuroku* [Meiji record of filial acts] (Tokyo: Kunaishō, 1877); Nishimura Shigeki, Yamada An'ei, and Kabe Iwao. *Fujo kagami* [Mirror of women] (Tokyo: Kunaisho, 1887).

49. Katano, *Kōgō no kindai*, 33–34.

50. Wakakuwa, *Kōgō no shōzō*, 153.

51. Wakakuwa, *Kōgō no shōzō*, 159.

52. Wakakuwa, *Kōgō no shōzō*, 334.

53. Shizuko Koyama, *Ryōsai Kenbo*.

54. Shizuko Koyama, *Ryōsai Kenbo*, 4–5.

55. Shizuko Koyama, *Ryōsai Kenbo*, 4–5.

56. Shizuko Koyama, *Ryōsai Kenbo*, 7.

57. Atsuko Sakaki, *Obsessions with the Sino-Japanese Polarity in Japanese Literature* (Honolulu: University of Hawai'i Press, 2006); Mari Nagase, "Women Writers of Chinese Poetry in Late-Edo Period Japan" (PhD diss., University of British Columbia, 2007); Suzuki Sadami, *The Concept of "Literature" in Japan*, trans. Royall Tyler (Kyoto: International Research Center for Japanese Studies, 2006), 128.

58. Hirata, *Josei hyōgen no Meijishi*, 21–23.

59. Mehl, "Women Educators," 580.

60. See P. K. Kornicki, "Women, Education, and Literacy," in *The Female as Subject: Reading and Writing in Early Modern Japan*, 25.

61. Sumiko Sekiguchi, "Confucian Morals and the Making of a 'Good Wife and Wise Mother': From 'Between Husband and Wife There Is Distinction' to 'As Husbands and Wives Be Harmonious,'" *Social Science Japan Journal* 13, no. 1 (2010): 95–113, 106.

62. Kajiwara Chikuken, *Wakae Nioko to Wage onna shishō* (Tokyo: Kagawa Shinpōsha, 1917), 38–41.

63. Mori Ōgai, "Tsuge Shirōzaemon," first published in *Chūō kōron* (Central review) 4 (1915).

64. Mori Ōgai, "Tsuge Shirōzaemon," in *Ōgai rekishi bungakushū* [Collection of Ōgai's literary historical works] (Tokyo: Iwanami Shoten, 1999), 3:127–73; David Dilworth and J. Thomas Rimer, eds., *The Historical Fiction of Mori Ōgai* (Honolulu: University of Hawai'i Press, 1991), 294.

65. Dilworth and Rimer, *Historical Fiction of Mori Ōgai*, 298–99.

66. Dilworth and Rimer, *Historical Fiction of Mori Ōgai*, 295.

67. Dilworth and Rimer, *Historical Fiction of Mori Ōgai*, 297.

68. *Shuridaibu* is the court title equivalent to "minister of works" or "chief of palace repairs."

69. Sally A. Hastings, "Women Educators of the Meiji Era and the Making of Modern Japan," *International Journal of Social Education* 6, no. 1 (1991): 83-94.

70. Hastings, "Women Educators," 579.

71. Meiji Jingū, *Shōken Kōtaigō jitsuroku*, 1:73, 216, 371.

72. Mehl, "Women Educators," 590.

73. Masuda Wataru, *Japan and China: Mutual Representations in the Modern Era*, trans. Joshua A. Fogel (London: RoutledgeCurzon, 2004), 82; Peter Kornicki, *The Book in Japan: A Cultural History from the Beginnings to the Nineteenth Century* (Honolulu: University of Hawai'i Press, 2001), 120

74. *Shimoda Utako sensei den* [Biography of Shimoda Utako] (Tokyo: Ko Shimoda Kōcho Sensei Denki Hensanjo, 1943), 18-29; Kornicki, *The Book in Japan*, 149.

75. *Shimoda Utako sensei den*, 94. Kindai had been appointed *Senkyōshi hakase* while Hirao had been appointed *shishō*.

76. *Sokoku Sento Jōji joshi chūgakkō kisoku* (undated translation of the rules of St. George's School for Girls, Edinburgh), Jissen Women's University Library, Shimoda Utako Archives, Tokyo.

77. Yamakawa Michiko, *Jokan*, 1-2.

78. The empress bequeathed two poems to the Peeresses' School, "*Kongōseki*" (Diamond) and "*Mizu wa utsuwa*" (Water in a vessel). Meiji Jingū, *Shoken Kotaigō jitsuroku* 1: 410-12. For a translation and discussion of "*Kongōseki*," see Keene, *Emperor of Japan*, 412.

79. Dorothy Ko, *Teachers of the Inner Chambers: Women and Culture in Seventeenth-Century China* (Stanford, CA: Stanford University Press, 1994), 8.

80. Wakakuwa, *Kōgō no shōzō*, 334.

81. Dorothy Ko, JaHyun Kim Haboush, and Joan R. Piggott, "Introduction," in *Women and Confucian Cultures in Premodern China, Korea, and Japan* (Berkeley: University of California Press, 2003), 3.

82. T. Fujitani, *Splendid Monarchy: Power and Pageantry in Modern Japan* (Berkeley: University of California Press, 1996), 26-27.

83. Wakakuwa, *Kōgō no shōzō*, 13.

Chapter 2

1. *Yomiuri shimbun* [Yomiuri newspaper], April 7, 1882, in Hirata, *Josei hyōgen no Meijishi*, 22. Emphasis is in the original.

2. From 1882 to 1883 various newspapers in the Osaka, Okayama, Shikoku, Kumamoto, and Kyoto areas reported on Kishida Toshiko's speeches. These include but are not limited to *Nihon Rikken Seitō shimbun, Sanyō shimbun, Futsū shimbun, Kumamoto shim-*

bun, Jiji shinpō, and *Asahi shimbun.* Articles are compiled in Nakajima Shōen, *Kishida Toshiko hyōronshū* [Kishida Toshiko essay collection], vol. 1 of *Shōen senshū* [Shōen's collected works] (Tokyo: Fuji Shuppan, 1985), 231–66.

3. Hirata, *Josei hyōgen no Meijishi,* 21–23.

4. Sharon L Sievers, *Flowers in Salt: The Beginnings of Feminist Consciousness in Modern Japan* (Stanford, CA: Stanford University Press, 1983). Anderson, *A Place in Public.*

5. The work has been translated by Dawn Elizabeth Lawson as "A Famous Flower in Mountain Seclusion," in Dawn Elizabeth Lawson, "Women, Creativity, and Translation in Mid-Meiji Japan: The Literature of Nakajima Shoen (1861–1901)" (PhD diss., New York University, 2014).

6. Copeland, *Lost Leaves.* Lawson, "Women, Creativity, and Translation in Mid-Meiji Japan."

7. Rebecca L. Copeland, *Woman Critiqued: Translated Essays on Japanese Women's Writing* (Honolulu: University of Hawai'i Press, 2006), 21.

8. Oguri Fūyō et al., "On Women Writers," trans. Rebecca L. Copeland, in *Woman Critiqued,* 33–40, 34.

9. Yosano Akiko, "What Is 'Womanliness'?" trans. Laurel Rasplica Rodd, in Copeland, *Woman Critiqued,* 40–46, 46.

10. Martha Tocco, "Made in Japan: Meiji Women's Education," in *Gendering Modern Japanese History,* ed. Barbara Molony and Kathleen Uno (Cambridge, MA: Harvard University Asia Center, 2005), 47.

11. Tocco, "Made in Japan," 47.

12. Tocco, "Made in Japan," 52.

13. *Genbun itchi* literally means "combined spoken and written." The *genbun itchi* movement aimed to make written prose closer to the Japanese spoken in the Tokyo area and was instrumental in the modernization of education and the literary arts in the Meiji period.

14. Sakaki, *Obsessions*; Rebecca L. Copeland and Melek Ortabasi, eds., *The Modern Murasaki: Writing by Women of Meiji Japan* (New York: Columbia University Press, 2006).

15. Saitō Mareshi, *Kanbunmyaku to kindai nihon,* 3.

16. Seki Reiko, *Kataru onnatachi no jidai: Ichiyō to Meiji josei hyōgen* [The era of narrating women: Ichiyō and the expression of Meiji Women] (Tokyo: Shinyosha, 1997), 16. These terms were first used by Kamo no Mabuchi (1697–1769), who used "*taoyame buri*" to refer dismissively to the poetic style of the *Kokin wakashū,* a collection of *waka* using Chinese characters. By contrast, he referred positively to the poetry of the *Manyōshū* as "*masurao buri*" because it used *kana.*

17. Sakaki, *Obsessions,* 113, 115.

18. Sakaki, *Obsessions,* 114.

19. Sakaki, *Obsessions,* 105.

20. Hideo Kamei, "The Transformability of Self-Consciousness: Fantasies of Self in

the Political Novel," trans. John Mertz, in *Transformations of Sensibility: The Phenomenology of Meiji Literature* (Ann Arbor: University of Michigan Press, 2002), 26.

21. Hideo Kamei, "Transformability of Self-Consciousness," 26.

22. Hideo Kamei, "Transformability of Self-Consciousness," 27.

23. Hideo Kamei, "Transformability of Self-Consciousness," 30.

24. Sakaki, *Obsessions*, 3.

25. Famous narratives of women "hiding" or obscuring their proficiency in classical Chinese have existed since the Heian period, although the moral evaluation of such figures like Sei Shōnagon and Murasaki Shikibu differs by era. Sei Shōnagon criticizes Murasaki Shikibu for too prominently hinting at her *kanbun* literacy in *The Pillow Book*.

26. N. Volosinov. *Marxism and the Philosophy of Language,* (New York: Seminar Press, 1973). 46.

27. 「兎も角我が母公に列れての遠遊は其情他人の酌量すべからざるものあり。」. *Fujo shinbun hihyō*, "Kōko no koe," 13.

28. Sakaki, *Obsessions*, 103-28.

29. Nishikawa Yūko, *Hana no imōto* [Younger sister of the flowers] (Tokyo: Shinchōsha, 1986), 8.

30. Sōma Kokkō, *Meiji shoki no sanjosei: Nakajima Shōen, Wakamatsu Shizuko, Shimizu Shikin*, 4th ed. (Tokyo: Fuji Shuppan, 1986), 28-29; Nishikawa, *Hana no imōto*, 8.

31. Margaret Mehl, *Private Academies of Chinese Learning in Meiji Japan: The Decline and Transformation of the* Kangaku Juku (Copenhagen: Nordic Institute of Asian Studies Press, 2003), 17.

32. Kyōtoshi Kyōiku Iinkai Kyōtoshi Gakkō Rekishi Hakubutsukan [Kyoto Educational Committee, Kyoto School Historical Museum], ed., *Kyōto gakkō monogatari* [The tale of Kyoto schools] (Kyoto: Kyoto Tsūshinsha, 2006), 46; Duke, *The History of Modern Japanese Education*, 71.

33. Mehl, *Private Academies of Chinese Learning in Meiji Japan*, 21.

34. Copeland, *Lost Leaves*, 11. See also Itō Toshiyuki and Kyoto-fu Kyōikukai, *Kyōto-fu kyōikushi jō; kōki nisen-roppyakunen kinen; Nihon kyōikushi bunken shūsei 1; Chihō kyōikushi no bu* [Educational history of Kyoto Prefecture I: 2600th anniversary of Jimmu; Collection of Japanese educational history documents; Regional History Edition] (Tokyo: Daiichi Shobō, 1983).

35. Students at *kangaku juku* (*juku* of Chinese learning) in Tokyo in the 1870s were in their mid-teens to late twenties. Margaret Mehl, *Private Academies of Chinese Learning in Meiji Japan*, 46-50.

36. Shōen and Soeda Juichi (1864-1929), the future banker and finance minister in the Okura Cabinet, were deemed the two prodigies (*jindō*) of Kyoto.

37. These works were part of the fourth-, fifth-, and sixth-year curriculum of the Kyoto public primary schools, which Shōen attended. Kyōtoshi Kyōiku Iinkai, ed., *Kyōto gakkō monogatari*, 88.

38. Saitō Mareshi, *Kanbunmyaku to kindai nihon*, 66, 91.

39. Copeland, *Lost Leaves*, 11. See also Itō Toshiyuki and Kyoto-fu Kyōikukai, *Kyō-to-fu kyōikushi jō*.

40. It is interesting to note that calligraphy was an "indispensible element in the education of the aristocracy" and, following classical Chinese tradition, that it was sought as a mirror of a ruler's character. Keene, *Emperor of Japan*, 46.

41. Previous ladies-in-waiting were recruited from the samurai class or were women of aristocratic lineage. Shōen entered service at the fifteenth rank. As a point of reference, the poet Shimoda Utako (1854–1936), who was a proponent of women's education and standards for their proper behavior—as reflected in the slogan coined by Masanao Nakamura in 1875, "good wife, wise mother"—also entered court at the fifteenth rank as a court poet and poetry advisor. Shimoda served from 1872 to 1879, until she left her post to marry.

42. Mehl, *Private Academies of Chinese Learning in Meiji Japan*, xii.

43. When she resigned, Shōen gave the customary excuse of illness as the reason for her departure, although she was likely leaving to marry. This marriage failed almost immediately when her in-laws rejected Shōen because they deemed her guilty of one or more of the seven justifications for divorcing a wife (*shichikyo*), which was explained in a letter they sent to her parents after Shōen returned to her natal family. The *shichikyo*, which are listed in Kaibara Ekiken's *Onna daigaku* (Greater learning for women), include disobeying one's parents-in-law, not bearing children, being promiscuous, envious, diseased, or outspoken, and stealing. Yokozawa Kiyoko, *Jiyū minkenka Nakajima Nobuyuki to Kishida Toshiko: Jiyū e no Tatakai* (Freedom and Popular Rights Activists Nakajima Nobuyuki and Kishida Toshiko: The Struggle Toward Freedom) (Tokyo: Akashi shoten, 2006), 254–255. Nishikawa Yūko, *Hongō dayori* 14 [Letters from Hongō 14] (Tokyo: Fuji Shuppan, 1996).

44. Nishikawa, *Hongō dayori*, 3; Shōen's *kanshi*, quoted in Sōma, *Meiji shoki no sanjosei*, 40–41, speak of the uneventful and luxurious lifestyle at court and contrast it with the famine and unrest publicized daily in newspapers.

45. For example, in 1882, some of Shōen's multiday events included speeches at Okayama Shinmeiza (Okayama Shinmei Theater), May 13–15; Tokushima Terashimachō Fushimiza (Terashima City Fushimi Theater), June 23–25; and Kumamoto Kuma-gun (Kumamoto Kuma district), November 10–12. Yokozawa, *Jiyū minkenka Nakajima Nobuyuki to Kishida Toshiko*, 271.

46. September 27, 1891. Nakajima Shōen, *Shōen nikki* [Shōen's diaries], ed. Ōki Motoko and Nishikawa Yūko, vol. 3 of *Shōen senshū* (Tokyo: Fuji Shuppan, 1986), 39.

47. Yao and Shun were legendary emperors of ancient China.

48. Nakajima Shōen, "Mudai" [Untitled], in *Kishida Toshiko bungakushū*, vol. 2 of *Shōen senshū* (Tokyo: Fuji Shuppan, 1985), 268. I would like to thank Robert Tuck and Fumiko Jōo for their guidance on the *kanshi* translations. All mistranslations are my own.

49. "Daughters in Boxes," in Copeland and Ortabasi, eds., *Modern Murasaki*, 62–71.

50. Jiyū Shimbun, October 1883, in *Kishida Toshiko hyōronshū*, 208.

51. *Nihon Rikken Seitō shimbun* no. 463, October 18, 1883, in *Kishida Toshiko hyōronshū*, 209.

52. *Nihon Rikken Seitō shimbun* no. 463, October 18, 1883, in *Kishida Toshiko hyōronshū*, 209.

53. Shōen, *Shōen nikki*, ed. Ishikawa Eiji and Fujii Tei (Tokyo: Ikuseikai, 1903), 171–72.

54. Ōki Motoko, *Jiyū minken undō to josei* (Tokyo: Domesu shuppan, 2004), 78.

55. Ōki Motoko, *Jiyū minken undō to josei*, 79.

56. The *Rikken Seitō shimbun* grew out of Furuzawa Shigeru's (1847–1911) acquisition of the *Osaka nippō* (Osaka daily report), a left-leaning Kansai paper, which Furuzawa turned into an organ of his party. The Pro-Constitution Party was a branch of the Jiyūtō (Liberal Party), founded by Itagaki Taisuke. Furuzawa had close ties with Itagaki, having worked with him in 1874 on the petition to found Aikokusha (Society of Patriots), a patriotic party protesting the Satcho-dominated government. While the *Rikken Seitō shimbun* was suspended numerous times, its predecessor, *Osaka nippō*, had not been subjected to the ban ordered by the 1883 press law. Thus, when *Rikken Seitō shimbun* was suspended, the *Osaka nippō* resurfaced to take its place. Unlike the *Jiyū shimbun* (Liberal newspaper), which folded when the Jiyūtō collapsed, the *Rikken Seitō shimbun* continued until 1887, despite the dissolution of its affiliated political party. Okano Takeo, *Meiji genronshi* (Tokyo: Hō Shuppan, 1974).

57. Morosawa Yoko, *Onna no rekishi*, vol. 3 (Tokyo: Miraisha, 1970), 80.

58. *Kishida Toshiko hyōronshū*, 220–21.

59. John Mertz, *Novel Japan: Spaces of Nationhood in Early Meiji Narrative, 1870–88* (Ann Arbor: University of Michigan Press, 2003), 117. Mertz cites the trial of Usui Rokurō, who in 1880 avenged his father, a mid-ranking domainal official, by killing his supposed murderer, Ichinose Naohisa. Ichinose was a former member of an ultranationalist society who, despite his misgivings toward modernization, found success as a judge following the Meiji Restoration in 1868.

60. Mertz, *Novel Japan*, 136. Mertz specifically refers to the political novels of the early and mid-1880s and to later novels such as Futabatei Shimei's *Ukigumo* (Floating clouds) and Ozaki Kōyō's *Konjiki yasha* (Golden demon).

61. Barbara Molony, "'The Quest for Women's Rights in Turn-of-the-Century Japan," in *Gendering Modern Japanese History*, ed. Molony and Uno, 463–92.

62. Shōen, *Shōen nikki* (1903).

63. Ōki Motoko, "Kaidai" [Precis], in Nakajima Shōen, *Shōen nikki*, 15. The full contents of the two final diaries, dating from 1899 to 1901, were published as *Shōen nikki* in 1903. Shōen's first five diary notebooks (1891–96) were not published until 1985–86, when the historians Ōki Motoko and Nishikawa Yūko compiled all seven extant diaries in a comprehensive collection of Shōen's writings with the same title, *Shōen nikki*, in the four-volume collection *Shōen senshū*, ed. Suzuki Yūko (Tokyo: Fuji Shuppan, 1986). Fol-

lowing Ōki and Nishikawa's example, I refer to all seven diary notebooks published in 1985–1986 (included the two already published in 1903), as *Shōen nikki*.

64. "Kōkō no koe" (Voices of the world) in reprint of *Shōen nikki* (1903), in Yamazaki, *Sōsho Joseiron* 2 (Tokyo: Ōzorasha, 1995), 1–23, 20.

65. "Kōkō no koe," 10.

66. "Kōkō no koe," 10.

67. "Kōkō no koe," 13.

68. [Tokutomi Sohō] Sohō Sei, "*Shōen nikki* o yomu," in *Kokumin shimbun*, May 10, 1903. Sohō's review also appears in an anthology of his writings: Tokutomi Sohō [Tokutomi Iichirō], *Dokusho yoroku* [Reading anecdotes] (Tokyo: Minyūsha, 1905).

69. Tokutomi, *Dokusho yoroku*, 98.

70. Tokutomi, *Dokusho yoroku*, 98.

71. Tokutomi, *Dokusho yoroku*, 105.

72. Tokutomi, *Dokusho yoroku*, 99.

73. Tokutomi, *Dokusho yoroku*, 99.

74. Michael K. Bourdaghs, *The Dawn That Never Comes: Shimazaki Tōson and Japanese Nationalism* (New York: Columbia University Press, 2003), 8–9.

75. "Kōkō no koe," 20.

76. Nobuyuki had married his first wife, Hatsuho, Mutsu Munemitsu's younger sister, in 1869. Hatsuho died at the age of twenty-eight, leaving behind three adolescent sons, whom Shōen later helped to raise.

77. Article 5 of the Security Police Law of 1900 (*Chian keisatsu hō*) "barred women from attending political meetings." See Anderson, *A Place in Public*, 147–48. Rumi Yasutake, *Transnational Women's Activism: The United States, Japan, and Japanese Immigrant Communities in California, 1859–1920* (New York: New York University Press, 2004), 66–67.

78. *Kokumin shimbun*, November 29, 1891, in Nakayama Yasumasa, ed., *Shimbun shūsei: Meiji hennenshi* [Chronological history of Meiji compiled from newspapers] 8 (Tokyo: Shimbun shūsei Meiji hennenshi Hensankai, 1936), 158. The article refers to her both by her *gagō* and the suffix referring to a female intellectual, "Shōen joshi" (Lady Shōen), and as "Nakajima gichō fujin" (Mrs. Speaker Nakajima, or Speaker Nakajima's wife).

79. November 28–29, 1891. Shōen, *Shōen nikki* (1986), 46.

80. November 28–29, 1891. Shōen, *Shōen nikki* (1986), 46.

81. November 28–29, 1891. Shōen, *Shōen nikki* (1986), 47.

82. "In the women's seats, we saw Mrs. Nakajima (Speaker Nakajima's spouse)." *Jiji shinpō*, December 1, 1891.

83. Shōen, *Shōen nikki* (1986), 58.

84. Historian J. Charles Schencking describes Kabayama's attitude toward Parliament as follows: the "hot-tempered and strong-willed navy minister felt that matters of military policy transcended the realm of party politics" and with his speech "crippled

the cabinet's attempts to secure support in parliament." He "contemptuously criticized Diet members for their rejection of the bill." This speech would later be called the "indignation speech." J. Charles Schencking, "The Politics of Pragmatism and Pageantry: Selling a National Navy at the Elite and Local Level in Japan, 1890–1913," in *Nation and Nationalism in Japan*, ed. Sandra Wilson (London: Routledge, 2002), 21–37, 23–25.

85. Nakajima Shōen, "Sankan no meika" [Noble flowers of the mountains], in *Kishida Toshiko bungakushū*, 165.

86. December 25, 1891. Shōen, *Shōen nikki* (1986), 62.

87. V. N. Voloshinov, *Marxism and the Philosophy of Language* (New York: Seminar Press, 1973), 46.

88. Shōen, *Shōen Nikki* (1903), 87.

89. *Yomiuri shimbun*, November 5, 1892.

90. *Yomiuri shimbun*, November 5, 1892.

91. September 27, 1892. Shōen, *Shōen nikki* (1986), 69.

92. Sugano Noriko, "Kishida Toshiko to *Onna Daigaku*," *Teikyō Shigaku* 25, no. 2 (2010): 67–107, 74.

93. December 3, 1891. Shōen, *Shōen nikki* (1986), 49.

94. November 15, 1896. Shōen, *Shōen nikki* (1986), 151.

95. Sōma, *Meiji shoki no sanjosei*, 23–27.

96. Sōma, *Meiji shoki no sanjosei*, 25.

97. Sōma, *Meiji shoki no sanjosei*, 26.

98. February 22, 1894. Shōen, *Shōen nikki* (1986), 106.

99. October 31, 1892. Nakajima Shōen, *Shōen nikki* (1986), 85–86.

100. November 29, 1892. Shōen, *Shōen nikki* (1986), 83. She makes reference to the fourth line of Meng Haoran's (689–740 CE) "Seeing Off Du Shishi as He Departs for Jiangnan."

101. March 20, 1901. Shōen, *Shōen nikki* (1986), 236.

102. In *Seinen kurabu* and *Jokan*, compiled in "Kōkō no koe," 15–18.

Chapter 3

1. In total the *Osaka Asahi* series *Jinbutsu gaden* (Pictorial record of notable persons) featured one hundred profiles, only five of whom were women, and of these, Utako's profile was the first to appear. The articles were later compiled in Gadenshi, ed., *Jinbutsu gaden* (Tokyo: Yūgakusha, 1907). Also quoted is Yamamoto Hiroo, "Kaisetsu 'Yōfu Shimoda Utako' mondai," in *Yōfu Shimoda Utako: Heimin shimbun yori* (Nagoya: Fūbosha, 1999), 222–46, 223. James Huffman writes that the paper had a readership of 123,566 in 1906. James Huffman, *Creating a Public: People and Press in Meiji Japan*. (Honolulu: University of Hawai'i Press, 1997), 317.

2. Gadenshi, ed., *Jinbutsu gaden*, 31–32, 31.

3. "Yōfu Shimoda Utako," *Heimin shimbun* (Tokyo), February 24, 1907–April 13, 1907. Fukao Shō (1883–1963) was widely thought to be the author of the series. Yamamoto, "Kaisetsu 'Yōfu Shimoda Utako' mondai," 237.

4. Huffman, *Creating a Public*, 339.

5. Huffman, *Creating a Public*, 328–36.

6. Huffman, *Creating a Public*, 349.

7. Huffman, *Creating a Public*, 328.

8. In 1887, during a masked ball hosted by Itō Hirobumi at his Nagatachō residence, the host allegedly raped the wife of Count Ujikata Toda, Ujikata Kiwako, who was also the eldest daughter of Iwakura Tomomi. Numerous newspapers covered this incident, one of the numerous sex scandals linked with the powerful statesman. It is alleged in *Heimin shimbun Yōfuden* no.8, March 3, 1907, that Utako may have lured the young woman for Itō's planned attack.

9. Jissen Women's University, "Heisei 26-nendo gakuseisū," accessed August 29, 2015, http://www.jissen.ac.jp/information_disclosure/02-01.html.

10. Joan Judge, *The Precious Raft of History: The Past, the West, and the Woman Question in China* (Stanford, CA: Stanford University Press, 2008), 111.

11. Copeland, *Lost Leaves*, 217.

12. Copeland, *Lost Leaves*, 217.

13. Jan Bardsley, "The New Woman Exposed: Redefining Women in Modern Japanese Photography," in *New Woman International: Representations in Photography and Film from the 1870s through the 1960s*, ed. Elizabeth Otto and Vanessa Rocco (Ann Arbor: University of Michigan Press, 2011), 42.

14. Ayako Kano, *Acting Like a Woman in Modern Japan: Theater, Gender, and Nationalism* (New York: Palgrave, 2001), 25.

15. Mehl, "Women Educators," 579.

16. Mehl, "Women Educators," 579.

17. Matsuda Wataru, *Japan and China*, 82. Kornicki, *The Book in Japan*, 120.

18. "Sono koro no Shimoda-sensei," transcribed interview with Motono Hisako, daughter of government official Motono Ichirō, in *Shimoda Utako sensei den*, 185–86.

19. Yamaguchi Teitarō, *Meiji Kōgō* (Tokyo: Nanbokusha, 1914), 106.

20. Around the time Utako first left court, her father, Hirao Jūzo, approached activist and writer Yamakawa Kikue's mother, Chise, for *kanshi* lessons for his daughter and lamented her mistreatment by her fellow court servants. Yamakawa Kikue, *Onna nidai no ki* (Tokyo: Nihon hyōronshinsha, 1956), 48–49.

21. Shimoda Utako, "Ōshū junkai gan" 『欧洲巡回願』 Kunai daijin Tsuchikata Hisamoto ate ("A Request to Travel to England" Letter addressed to Interior Minister Tsuchikata Hisamoto). August 19, 1893. Shimoda Utako Archive. Jissen Women's Library, Jissen Women's University.

22. The library formed the core of what would become the Tokyo Municipal Hibiya Library in 1908 (now Tokyo Metropolitan Library). On Elizabeth Anna Gordon, see Noboru Koyama, "Cultural Exchange at the Time of the Anglo-Japanese Alliance," in *The Anglo-Japanese Alliance, 1902–1922*, ed. Phillips Payson O'Brien (London: RoutledgeCurzon, 2004), 203–6.

23. Ozeki Keiko, "*61 Princes Gate* to *19 Pelham Place*: Shimoda Utako no Rondon shakujūkyo," *Jissen joshi daigaku bungaku kiyō* 56 (2014): 1–12. At the time, Utako lived with the forty-eight-year-old Edwards and her daughter.

24. Shimoda, *Taisei fujo fūzoku* [Customs of western women] (Tokyo: Dai Nihon Jogakkai, 1899), 189.

25. "Teikoku fujin kyōkai shushi tekiyō," *Shimoda Utako sensei den*, 335. Utako also recorded her experiences and observations of this sojourn in the instructional *Taisei fujo fūzoku*, a five-volume collection of writings that had been published between 1932 and 1934, and in her memoir "Soto no hamazuto" [Souvenirs from abroad], in *Kōsetsu sōsho* (Tokyo: Jissen Jogakko Shuppanbu, 1932), 188–295.

26. *Shimoda Utako sensei den*, 258. She stopped along the way briefly in Quebec, Canada, and the United States and arrived back in Japan on August 20, 1895.

27. *Shimoda Utako sensei den*, 345.

28. *Shimoda Utako sensei den*, 358.

29. *Shimoda Utako sensei den*, 361–62.

30. *Shimoda Utako sensei den*, 338. Shimoda writes *"infuruensu"* in parentheses as a gloss for *kanka*.

31. *Shimoda Utako sensei den*, 193.

32. In addition, she founded the Women's School for the Industrial Arts; formed the Niigata branch of the Imperial Women's Association; founded and served as principal of the affiliate sewing training school, later the Niigata School for the Industrial Arts (currently Niigata Seiryō University); served as instructor and dean of the Gakushūin women's division; established and directed the Imperial Women's Association (Teikoku Fujin Kyōkai), also creating an affiliate kindergarten at which she served as director; and acted as director and principal of Junshin Girls' School (Junshin jogakkō).

33. Katayama Seiichi, *Kindai Nihon no joshi kyōiku* (Tokyo: Kenpakusha, Showa 59, 1984).

34. Wm. Theodore de Bary, Ryusaku Tsunoda, and Donald Keene, eds., *Sources of Japanese Tradition* (New York: Columbia University Press, 1964), 2: 522, 137.

35. Yoshida Kumaji, "Gakusei" [Fundamental code for education], in *Monbushō futatsu*, vol. 13 (Tokyo, 1872).

36. Carol Gluck, *Japan's Modern Myths: Ideology in the Late Meiji Period* (Princeton, NJ: Princeton University Press, 1987), 121.

37. Gluck, *Japan's Modern Myths*, 120–27.

38. Katayama, *Kindai Nihon no joshi kyōiku*, 50–51.

39. Katayama, *Kindai Nihon no joshi kyōiku*, 44–49.

40. Masuko Honda, *Jogakusei No Keifu: Saishikisareru Meiji* (Tokyo: Seikyusha, 1990), 65.

41. Melanie Czarnecki, "Bad Girls from Good Families: The Degenerate Meiji Schoolgirl," in *Bad Girls of Japan*, ed. Laura Miller and Jan Bardsley (New York: Palgrave Macmillan, 2005), 49–64, 61.

42. Shimoda Utako, "Jogakusei no daraku mondai ni tsuite" [On the problem of schoolgirls' degeneracy], *Yomiuri shimbun*, November 2–8, 1902.

43. Shimoda Utako, "Joshi kyōiku no shotaika no danwa" [Conversations with leaders of women's education], *Yomiuri shimbun*, no. 15–19, November 2, 4, 5, 6, 8, 1902.

44. Honda, *Jogakusei No Keifu*, 63.

45. Honda, *Jogakusei No Keifu*, 65.

46. Honda, *Jogakusei No Keifu*, 119.

47. Ebara, "Meiji ikō no kango no keimō kyōiku," 121. Judge, *The Precious Raft of History*. Helen M. Schneider, *Keeping the Nation's House: Domestic Management and the Making of Modern China* (Vancouver: University of British Columbia Press, 2011).

48. Ebara Junko, "Meiji ikō no kango no keimō kyōiku: 'Katei Kangosho' no henkan wo tōshite," *Niigata Seiryō Daigaku Kiyō* 7, no. 3 (2007): 118.

49. Ebara Junko, "Meiji ikō no kango no keimō kyōiku," 116; Schneider, *Keeping the Nation's House*, 86.

50. Obie Fumiko and Ishii Noriko, "Shimoda Utako no Shomotsu ni miru Meiji/Taishōjidai no 'Katei kango,'" *Akita Daigaku Igakubu Hokengakka Kiyō* 12, no. 2 (2004): 108.

51. Of Utako's publications, the domestic science textbooks written for use in the Jissen Higher Specialized School were meant for a small group of students, although they were available by mail order. While several English-language domestic science textbooks had been translated into Japanese, Shimoda Utako's *Kaseigaku* was considered the first written by a Japanese woman. Yamamoto, "Kaisetsu 'Yōfu Shimoda Utako' mondai," 225.

52. Shimoda, *Taisei fujo fūzoku*, 196.

53. Shimoda, *Taisei fujo fūzoku*, 196.

54. Shimoda, *Taisei fujo fūzoku*, 189.

55. *Genji monogatari kōgi: shukan* [The tale of Genji lectures: First volume] (Tokyo: Jissen jogakkō shuppanbu, 1936); *Genji monogatari ikkan: Kiritsubo, Hahakigi, Utsusemi* [The tale of Genji vol. 1: Kiritsubo, Hahakigi, Utsusemi] (Tokyo: Jissen jogakkō shuppanbu, 1936). These two volumes of Shimoda's writings and lecture materials on *Genji monogatari* appeared as the two additional volumes to *Kōsetsu sōsho*.

56. Shimoda, "Shogen (preface)," in *Genji monogatari kōgi: shukan*, 1.

57. Shimoda, *Genji monogatari kōgi: shukan*, 3.

58. Shimoda, *Genji monogatari kōgi: shukan*, 2.

59. Shimoda, *Genji monogatari kōgi: shukan*, 4.

60. Jan Bardsley, *The Bluestockings of Japan: New Woman Essays and Fiction from Seitō, 1911–16* (Ann Arbor: Center for Japanese Studies, University of Michigan, 2007), 1.

61. Tomida Hiroko, *Hiratsuka Raichō and Early Japanese Feminism* (Leiden, Netherlands: Brill, 2004), 145.

62. Tomida Hiroko, *Hiratsuka Raichō and Early Japanese Feminism*, 161.

63. Tomida Hiroko, *Hiratsuka Raichō and Early Japanese Feminism*, 183.

64. Bardsley, *The Bluestockings of Japan*, 4.

65. Ikuta Hanayo, "Taberu koto to teisō to," *Hankyō* 1, no. 5 (September 1914): 33–38, reproduced in Orii Miyako, ed., *Shiryō: Sei to ai o meguru rōnsō* [Sources: Debates about sex and love] (Tokyo: Domesu Shuppan, 1991), 13–18.

66. Isomura Haruko, *Ima no onna* (Tokyo: Bunmeidō, 1913), 169.

67. Ellen Key, *The Morality of Woman, and Other Essays*, trans. Mamah Bouton Borthwick (Chicago: Ralph Fletcher Seymour, 1911). Translated by Homma Hisao as *Fujin to dōtoku* (Tokyo: Nambokusha, 1913).

68. While we cannot assume that Utako was familiar with Key's work or with its translation, morality (*dōtoku*) was one of the main issues of contention among Bluestockings members and was what Utako saw as separating New Women from Old-Fashioned Women.

69. Itō Noe, "Shimoda Utako e," *Teihon Itō Noe Zenshū 2: Hyōron, zuihitsu, shokan 1*—Seitō *no jidai* (Tokyo: Gakugei Shorin, 2000), 114–18. Originally published in *Seitō* 4, no. 9 (October 1914): 117–18.

70. Kamichika Ichiko, "Shimoda Utako joshi yuku," Onna no tachibakara, *Yomiuri shimbun*, October 14, 1936, 9.

71. Kamichika Ichiko, "Shimoda Utako joshi yuku," 118.

72. Katayama, *Kindai Nihon no joshi kyōiku*, 160.

73. Key, *The Morality of Woman*, 62.

74. Vera Mackie, *Creating Socialist Women in Japan: Gender, Labour and Activism, 1900–1937* (Cambridge: Cambridge University Press, 2002), 41.

75. Judith Butler, *Excitable Speech: A Politics of the Performative* (New York: Routledge, 1997), 5.

76. Butler, *Excitable Speech*, 5.

77. *Yōfu Shimoda Utako, Heimin shimbun*, February 28, 1907–March 2, 1907.

78. *Heimin shimbun*, March 2, 1907. Reprinted in *Yōfu Shimoda Utako: Heimin shimbun yori*, 36.

79. Fukao Shō was a socialist former schoolteacher from Shizuoka Prefecture. He had worked alongside Sakai Toshihiko at the weekly *Heimin* newspaper before working at the daily *Heimin shimbun* with Sakai. A former coworker at the weekly paper, Arahata Kanson, confirmed Fukao's authorship of the series. Yamamoto, "Kaisetsu 'Yōfu Shimoda Utako' mondai," 237.

80. Susan Ehrlich, *Representing Rape: Language and Sexual Consent* (London: Routledge, 2001), 12.

81. J. L. Austin, *How to Do Things with Words*, ed. J. O. Urmson and Marina Sbisà, 2d ed. (Cambridge, MA: Harvard University Press, 2003), 6–7.

82. Yamamoto, "Kaisetsu 'Yōfu Shimoda Utako' mondai."

83. Yamamoto, "Kaisetsu 'Yōfu Shimoda Utako' mondai," 223.

84. Yamamoto, "Kaisetsu 'Yōfu Shimoda Utako' mondai," 223.

85. Marran, *Poison Woman*, 37, 64.

86. Uchida Roan, "Josensei," *Taiyō* [Sun] 9:3 (March 1903). Roan, along with figures like the literary critic and novelist Yamada Bimyō (1868–1910), was one of the first modern Japanese literary critics. He published widely in literary journals and newspapers, including *Jogaku zasshi*, the first general magazine *Kokumin no tomo* (The nation's friend), and *Mainichi shimbun* (Mainichi newspaper); he also drew attention to new writers like those involved in the Kenyūsha (Friends of the Inkstone) literary group, led

by the romantic realist writer Ozaki Kōyō (1867–1903), which experimented with new literary styles to promote the literary profession. Roan's translations of Western novels by Fyodor Dostoyevsky, Leo Tolstoy, Émile Zola, and Charles Dickens influenced many Japanese writers of the Meiji period.

87. Uchida, "Josensei," 76–77.

88. Uchida, "Josensei," 88.

89. Uchida, "Josensei," 93–94.

90. Uchida, "Josensei," 112.

91. Uchida, "Josensei," 128.

92. Uchida Roan, *Ikamono* [Imposter] (Tokyo: Kanao Bun'endō, 1909); Yi Sunshin, "'Josensei' to Shimoda Utako: 'Daraku Jogakusei' No Hyōshō, Moderu Mondai O Megutte," in *Honyaku No Ken'iki: Bunka, Shokuminchi, Aidentiti-*, ed. Tsukuba Daigaku Bunka Hihyō Kenkyūkai [The Tsukuba University Cultural Critique Research Group] (Tokyo: Isebu, 2004), 153–73.

93. For more on *Makaze koikaze*, see Czarnecki, "Bad Girls from Good Families," 54–57.

94. Uchida Roan, "Nihon ni okeru fujin mondai" [Women's issues in Japan], *Chuō Kōron, Rinji zōkan, fujin mondai gō* (1913): 7, cited in Katayama, *Kindai Nihon no joshi kyōiku*, 166–67.

BIBLIOGRAPHY

Periodicals

Jiji shimpō [Current events]
Jiyū shimbun [Freedom newspaper]
Heimin shimbun [Commoners' newspaper]
Nihon Rikken Seitō shimbun [Newspaper for the Constitutional Progressive Party], 1882–85
Yomiuri shimbun [Yomiuri newspaper]

Japanese Sources

Atomi Kakei. *Atomi Kakei nikki* [Atomi Kakei's diaries]. Tokyo: Atomi Gakuen, 2005–7.
Chō Tsurahiro, and Kosugi Sugimura. *Heian Kamakura jidai keishū nikkibun* [Women's diaries from the Heian and Kamakura periods]. Tokyo: Meikō Shoin, 1901.
Ebara Junko. "Meiji ikō no kango no keimō kyōiku: 'Katei kangosho' no henkan wo tōshite" [Home nursing as "enlightenment" education in the Meiji period: Examining 'home nursing guides']. *Niigata Seiryō Daigaku Kiyō* 7, no. 3 (2007): 115–29.
Ebihara Hachirō. "Meiji zasshi kaidai" [Bibliography of Meiji journals]. *Gekkan nihon bungaku* [Japanese literature monthly] 2, no. 4 (1932): 25.
Hayashi Mariko. *Mikado no onna*. Tokyo: Shinchōsha, 1990.
Higuchi Ichiyō. *Higuchi Ichiyō nikki* [Higuchi Ichiyō's diaries]. Edited by Suzuki Jun and Higuchi Tomoko. Tokyo: Iwanami Shoten, 2002.
Higuchi Ichiyō. *Ichiyō zenshū* [Complete works of Ichiyō]. Tokyo: Hakubunkan, 1912.
Hirata Yumi. *Josei hyōgen no Meijishi: Higuchi Ichiyo izen* [Women's expression as Meiji history: Before Higuchi Ichiyō]. Tokyo: Iwanami Shoten, 1999.
Hirotsu Ryūrō. "Joshi sansei shinchūrō" [The mirage of women's suffrage]. In *Meiji bunka zenshū* [Anthology of Meiji culture], vol. 22, Shakai hen [Society edition], 235–27. Tokyo: Nihon Hyōronsha, 1993.

Inoue Hisashi. "Ebichamurasaki no haha" [Mother of Ebichamurasaki]. In *Airōmono* (Inmate), 159–212. Tokyo: Bunshun bunkō, 1986.

Irokawa Daikichi. *Jiyū minken* [The Freedom and People's Rights Movement]. Tokyo: Iwanami Shinsho, 1981.

Ishida Hitoshi. "Nakajima Shōen 'Sankan no meika' ron" [On Nakajima Shōen's "Noble flowers of the mountains"]. *Bungaku ronsō: Tōyō daigaku bungakubu kiyō* [Literary debate: Tōyō University Literature Department bulletin] 73, no. 3 (1999): 21–40.

Isomura Haruko, and Isomura Eiichi. *Ima no onna*. Tokyo: Yūzankaku Shuppan, 1984.

Itō Chiyū. "Joketsu: Shōen joshi" [The heroine: Lady Shōen]. In *Itō Chiyū zenshū zoku* [Complete works of Itō Chiyū continued], vol. 8, edited by Itō Miyoji, Den Kenjirō, Gotō Shinpei, 138–50. Tokyo: Heibonsha, 1931.

Itō Noe. "Shimoda Utako e" [To Shimoda Utako]. In *Teihon Itō Noe zenshū* [Revised edition of the complete works of Itō Noe], vol. 2, *Hyōron, zuihitsu, shokan* [Criticism, essays, letters], pt. 1, *'Seitō' no jidai* [The Bluestockings era], 114–18. Tokyo: Gakugei Shorin, 2000.

Itō Toshiyuki, and Kyoto-fu Kyōikukai, *Kyōto-fu kyōikushi jō; kōki nisen-roppyakunen kinen; Nihon kyōikushi bunken shūsei* 1; Chihō kyōikushi no bu [Educational history of Kyoto Prefecture I: 2600th anniversary of Jimmu; Collection of Japanese educational history documents; Regional History Edition]. Tokyo: Daiichi Shobō, 1983.

Kaibara Ekiken. *Onna daigaku* [Greater learning for women]. Otsu: Shimabayashi Senjiro, 1883.

Kamei Hideo. *Meiji bungakushi* [Meiji literary history]. Tokyo: Iwanami Shoten, 2000.

Kamei Hideo. "Seiji e no kitai ga kuzureru toki: 'Joshi sansei shinchūrō' ron" [When hope in politics crumbles: On "The Mirage of Women's Suffrage"]. *Nihon kindai bungaku* [Modern Japanese literature] 25, no. 10 (1978): 76–84.

Kami Shōichirō, and Yamazaki Tomoko. *Nihon joseishi sōsho: Meiji Taishō-ki* [Japan women's history series: The Meiji and Taishō eras]. Tokyo: Kuresu Shuppan, 2008.

Kami Shōichirō, and Yamazaki Tomoko. *Nihon joseishi sōsho: Shōwa-ki* [Japan women's history series: The Shōwa era]. Tokyo: Kuresu Shuppan, 2008.

Kamichika Ichiko. "Shimoda Utako joshi yuku" [Shimoda Utako dies], Onna no tachibakara [From a woman's perspective]. *Yomiuri shimbun*, October 14, 1936.

Kan Satoko. *Onna ga kokka o uragiru toki: Jogakusei, Ichiyō, Yoshiya Nobuko* [When women betray the nation: Schoolgirls, Ichiyō, Yoshiya Nobuko]. Tokyo: Iwanami Shoten, 2011.

Kan Satoko. "Shōen nikki: Ware-Kimi no shōtenchi" [Shōen's diaries: The mini-universe of "I and He"]. *Kokubungaku: Kaishaku to kanshō* [National literature: Commentary and appreciation] 41, no. 2 (1996): 48–53.

Katano Masako. "Kindai kōgōzō no keisei" [The construction of the image of the modern empress]. In *Kindai Tennōsei no keisei to Kirisutokyō* [The construction of modern imperial ideology and Christianity], 79–132. Tokyo: Shinkyō shuppansha, 1996.

Katano Masako. *Kōgō no kindai* [The empress's modernity]. Tokyo: Kodansha, 2003.

Katayama Seiichi. *Kindai Nihon no joshi kyōiku* [Women's education in modern Japan]. Tokyo: Kenpakusha, 1984.

Key, Ellen Karolina Sofia. *Fujin to dōtoku* [Women and morality]. Translated by Honma Hisao. Tokyo: Nanbokusha, 1913.

Kishida Toshiko. *Hakoiri musume; Konin no fukanzen* [Cosseted daughters; The deficiencies of marriage]. Tokyo: Shinshindō, 1883.

Kishida Toshiko. *See also* Nakajima Shōen.

Kitada Sachie. *Kaku onnatachi: Edo kara Meiji no media bungaku jendā o yomu* [Writing women: Reading media, literature, and gender from the Edo to Meiji periods]. Tokyo: Gakugei Shorin, 2007.

Kitada Sachie. "Nakajima Shōen 'Sankan no meika' ron: Joken shōsetsu to shite no ichi" [On Nakajima Shōen's "Noble flowers of the mountains": Its position as a women's rights novel]. *Shakai bungaku* [Social literature] 1 (1987): 15–26.

Kondō Yoshiki. *Meiji Kōsetsuroku* [Meiji record of filial acts]. Tokyo: Kunaishō, 1877.

Kurita Shintarō. *Meiji enzetsu hyōbanki: Jiyū kaishin zenshin hoshu* [Compiled rankings of Meiji speakers: Liberal, Progressive, and Conservative parties]. Tokyo: Henryōkaku, 1882.

Kyōikushi Hensankai. *Meiji ikō kyōiku seido hattatsushi* [History of the development of the educational system since the Meiji period]. Tokyo: Kyōiku Shiryō Chōsakai, 1964–65.

Kyōtoshi Kyōiku Iinkai Kyōtoshi Gakkō Rekishi Hakubutsukan [Kyoto Educational Committee, Kyoto School Historical Museum], ed., *Kyōto gakkō monogatari* [The tale of Kyoto schools]. Kyoto: Kyoto Tsūshinsha, 2006.

Maeda Ai. "Shimoda Utako." In *Maeda Ai Chosakushū* [Collected works of Maeda Ai], vol. 3, Higuchi Ichiyō no sekai [The world of Higuchi Ichiyō]. Tokyo: Chikuma Shobō, 1989.

Mill, John Stuart. *Jiyū no kotowari*. 6 vols. Translated by Nakamura Keiū. Shizuoka: Kihira Ken'ichirō, 1871. Originally published as *On Liberty*. London: John W. Parker and Son, 1859.

Miura Kanō. *Meiji no kangaku* [Chinese studies of the Meiji period]. Tokyo: Kyūko shoin, 1998.

Monbushō futatsu zensho, Meiji 6-nen [Complete collection of the administrative orders of the Education Ministry, Meiji 6]. 1873.

Mori Ōgai, "Tsuge Shirōzaemon," *Ōgai rekishi bungakushū* [Collection of Ōgai's literary historical works], vol. 3, Sanshō ujo, Gyogenki, Takasebune yori [From "Salamander," "Gyogenki," "The Boat on the River Takase"]. Tokyo: Iwanami Shoten, 1999.

Morosawa Yoko. *Onna no rekishi* [Women's history]. 2 vols. Tokyo: Miraisha, 1970.

Murakami Nobuhiko. *Meiji joseishi* [Meiji women's history]. 4 vols. Tokyo: Rironsha, 1969–72.

Murasaki Shikibu. *Murasaki Shikibu nikki* [Murasaki Shikibu's diaries]. Niigata: Fujii Monpei, 1893.

Naitō Chizuko. *Teikoku to ansatsu: Jendā kara miru kindai Nihon no media hensei* [Empire and assassination: Examining modern Japan's organization of the media from the perspective of gender]. Tokyo: Shinyōsha, 2005.

Nakajima Shōen. *See also* Kishida Toshiko.

Nakajima Shōen. "Goku no kidan" [Prison narrative]. In *Shōen nikki* [Shōen's diaries], edited by Ōki Motoko and Nishikawa Yūko, 21–32. Vol. 3 of *Shōen senshū* [Shōen's collected works], edited by Suzuki Yūko. Tokyo: Fuji Shuppan, 1986.

Nakajima Shōen. *Kishida Toshiko bungakushū* [Kishida Toshiko literature edition]. Edited by Suzuki Yūko. Vol. 2 of *Shōen senshū* [Shōen's collected works], edited by Suzuki Yūko. Tokyo: Fuji Shuppan, 1985.

Nakajima Shōen. *Kishida Toshiko hyōronshū* [Kishida Toshiko essay collection]. Edited by Suzuki Yūko. Vol. 1 of *Shōen senshū* [Shōen's collected works], edited by Suzuki Yūko. Tokyo: Fuji Shuppan, 1985.

Nakajima Shōen. "Sankan no meika" [Noble flowers of the mountains]. In *Kishida Toshiko bungakushū*, edited by Suzuki Yūko, 121–175. Vol. 1 of *Shōen senshū* [Shōen's collected works], edited by Suzuki Yūko. Tokyo: Fuji Shuppan, 1985.

Nakajima Shōen. *Shōen nikki* [Shōen's diaries]. Edited by Ishikawa Eiji and Fujii Tei. Tokyo: Ikuseikai, 1903. This contains the full entries of the two final diary volumes, dating 1899–1901.

Nakajima Shōen. *Shōen nikki* [Shōen's diaries]. Edited by Ōki Motoko and Nishikawa Yūko. Vol. 3 of *Shōen senshū* [Shōen's collected works], edited by Suzuki Yūko. Tokyo: Fuji Shuppan, 1986. This contains all seven extant diaries: the first five notebooks (1891–96) published here for the first time and the two final diary volumes (1899–1901) published in 1903.

Nakajima Shōen. *Shōen senshū* [Shōen's collected works]. 4 vols. Tokyo: Fuji Shuppan, 1985–1986.

Nakayama Yasumasa, ed. *Shimbun shūsei Meiji hennenshi* [Chronological history of the Meiji period compiled from newspapers], vol. 8, Kokkai yōranki [Diet Infancy Period]. Tokyo: Shimbun shūsei Meiji hennenshi Hensankai, 1936.

Nishikawa Yūko. *Hana no imōto* [Younger sister of the flowers]. Tokyo: Shinchōsha, 1986.

Nishikawa Yūko. "Kaisetsu" [Analysis]. In Nakajima Shōen, *Shōen nikki* [Shōen's diaries], edited by Ōki Motoko and Nishikawa Yūko, 9–12. Vol. 3 of *Shōen senshū* [Shōen's collected works], edited by Suzuki Yūko. Tokyo: Fuji Shuppan, 1986.

Nishikawa Yūko. "Kishida Toshiko shinshiryō ni tsuite" [On new Kishida Toshiko documents], *Hongō dayori* [Letters from Hongō], no. 14, 1–6. Tokyo: Fuji Shuppan, 1986.

Nishimura Shigeki, Yamada An'ei, and Kabe Iwao. *Fujo kagami* [Mirror of women]. Kunaisho, 1887.

Obie Fumiko, and Ishii Noriko. "Shimoda Utako no shomotsu ni miru Meiji–Taishōjidai no 'katei kango'" [Meiji- and Taishō-era "home nursing" as found in the writings of Shimoda Utako]. *Akita Daigaku Igakubu Hokengakka Kiyō* 12, no. 2 (2004): 105–13.

Okano Takeo. *Meiji genronshi* [The history of the Meiji press]. Tokyo: Ōtori Shuppan, 1974.

Ōki Motoko. *Jiyū minken undō to josei* [The Freedom and People's Rights Movement and women]. Tokyo: Domesu Shuppan, 2003.

Ōki Motoko. "Kaidai" [Precis]. In Nakajima Shōen, *Shōen nikki* [Shōen's diaries], edited by Ōki Motoko and Nishikawa Yūko, 13–20. Vol. 3 of *Shōen senshū* [Shōen's collected works], edited by Suzuki Yūko. Tokyo: Fuji Shuppan, 1986.

Osaka Asahi Shimbunsha. *Jinbutsu gaden* [Pictorial record of notable persons]. Tokyo: Yūrakusha, 1907.

Ozeki Keiko. "*61 Princes Gate* to *19 Pelham Place*: Shimoda Utako no Rondon shakujū-kyo" [61 Princes Gate and 19 Pelham Place: Shimoda Utako's residences in London]. *Jissen joshi daigaku bungaku kiyō* 56 (2014): 1–12.

Saitō Mareshi. *Kanbunmyaku to kindai Nihon: Mō hitotsu no kotoba no sekai* [*Kanbunmyaku* and modern Japan: Another world of language]. Tokyo: Nihon Hōsō Shuppan Kyōkai, 2007.

Satō Eizō, ed. *Hanai Umejo kōhan bōchō hikki* [The public trial transcript of Hanai Ume]. Tokyo: Seibundō, 1880. Reprinted in Iwami Teruyo, *Hanai Ume-jo kōhan bōchō hikki: Fujin no hanzai ni kansuru kenkyū to gyōkeijō oyobi shakuhōgo ni okeru jissai teki kōsatsu* [The public trial transcript of Hanai Ume: A practical review of research pertaining to women's crimes and to the administration of punishment and matters following release], 1–44. Tokyo: Yumani Shobō, 2007.

Seki Reiko. *Ichiyō igo no josei hyōgen: Sutairu, media, jendā* [Women's expression after Ichiyō: Style, media, and gender]. Tokyo: Kanrin Shobō, 2003.

Seki Reiko. *Kataru onnatachi no jidai: Ichiyō to Meiji josei hyōgen* [The era of narrating women: Ichiyō and Meiji women's expression]. Tokyo: Shinyōsha, 1997.

Sekiguchi Sumiko. "Enzetsu suru onnatachi (sono 3): 'Meiji nijū sannen' no yume to joken shōsetsu" [Public speaking women, part 3: The dream of Meiji 23 and women's rights fiction]. *Mirai* [Future] 401 (1999): 14–20.

Sekiguchi Sumiko. *Goisshin to jendā: Ogyū Sorai kara Kyōiku chokugo made* [The Meiji Restoration and gender: From Ōgyū Sorai to the Imperial Rescript on Education]. Tokyo: Tokyo Daigaku Shuppankai, 2005.

Sekiguchi Sumiko. *Ryōsai kenbo shugi kara hazureta hitobito: Shōen, Raichō, Sōseki* [Those who fell away from the "good wife wise mother" ideology: Shōen, Raichō, Sōseki]. Tokyo: Misuzu Shobō, 2014.

Shimizu Takichi. *Kageyama Hidejo no den: Jiyū no gisei joken no kakuchō* [The story of Kageyama Hide: The sacrifice for freedom, the spread of women's rights]. Tokyo: Eisendō, 1887.

Shimoda Kageki. *Hana no arashi: Meiji no jotei, Shimoda Utako no ai to yabō* [Flower storm: The Meiji imperial woman, Shimoda Utako's love and ambition]. Tokyo: PHP Kenkyūjo, 1984.Shimoda Utako. *Genji monogatari ikkan: Kiritsubo, Hahakigi, Utsusemi* [The tale of Genji vol. 1: Kiritsubo, Hahakigi, Utsusemi]. Tokyo: Jissen jogakkō shuppanbu, 1936.

Shimoda Utako. *Genji monogatari kōgi: shukan* [The tale of Genji lectures: Vol. 1]. Tokyo: Jissen jogakkō shuppanbu, 1936.

Shimoda Utako. *Kosetsu sōsho: Shimoda Utako chosakushu* [The Snow White Flower series: Collected works of Shimoda Utako]. Vol. 1. Tokyo: Jissen Jogakko Shuppanbu, 1932.

Shimoda Utako. *Taisei fujo fūzoku* [Women's customs of the present day]. Tokyo: Dai Nihon jogakkai, 1899.

Shimoda Utako, ed. *Wabun kyōkasho* [Japanese writing textbook]. Tokyo: Chūōdō, 1886.

Shimoda Utako senseiden [Biography of Shimoda Utako]. Tokyo: Ko Shimoda Kōchō Sensei Denki Hensanjo, 1943.

Shioda Ryōhei. *Meiji joryū sakkaron* [The discourse of Meiji women authors]. Tokyo: Neiraku Shobō, 1965.

Shōken Kōtaigō jitsuroku [Authentic accounts of Empress Dowager Shōken]. Tokyo: Yoshikawa Kobunkan, 2014.

Sōma Kokkō. *Meiji shoki no sanjosei: Nakajima Shōen, Wakamatsu Shizuko, Shimizu Shikin* [Three women of the early Meiji period: Nakajima Shōen, Wakamatsu Shizuko, Shimizu Shikin]. Tokyo: Fuji Shuppan, 1985. First published in 1940 by Kōseikaku.

Spencer, Herbert. *Joken shinron* [True arguments for women's rights]. Translated by Inoue Tsutomu. Tokyo: Shiseidō, 1881. Originally published as *Social Statics; or, The Conditions Essential to Human Happiness Specified* (London: John Chapman, 1851).

Sugano Noriko. "'Kishida Toshiko to Onna Daigaku.'" *Teikyō Shigaku* 25, no. 2 (2010): 67–107.

Takada Chinami, Nakagawa Shigemi, and Nakayama Kazuko, eds. *Josei sakka shū* [Collection of women writers]. Tokyo: Iwanami Shoten, 2002.

Tanikawa Eichi. "Hirotsu Ryūrō 'Joshi sansei shinchūrō' no ichi" [The position of Hirotsu Ryūrō's "The Mirage of Women's Suffrage"]. *Nihon kindai bungaku* [Modern Japanese literature] 52, no. 11 (1983): 1–16.

Tōjō Kindai and Itō Keishū. *Shōgaku hitsudoku onna sanjikyo* [Elementary required reading Women's Three Character Classic]. Tokyo: Kyūkodō, 1873.

Tōkai Sanshi. *Kajin no kigū* [Chance encounters with beautiful women]. In *Meiji seiji shōsetsushū* [Collection of Meiji political novels]. Vol. 2, edited by Yanagida Izumi, 85–252. Tokyo: Chikuma Shobō, 1967.

Tokutomi Sohō [Tokutomi Iichirō]. *Dokusho yoroku* [Reading anecdotes]. Tokyo: Minyūsha, 1905.

Tokutomi Sohō [Sohō Sei]. "*Shōen nikki* o yomu." *Kokumin shimbun* [The nation's newspaper], May 10, 1903.

Tozuka Matsuko. *Kindai Nihon jokenshi* [Modern Japanese women's rights]. Tokyo: Ōzorasha, 1996.

Tsubouchi Shōyo, and Futabatei Shimei. *Tsubouchi Shōyō Futabatei Shimei shū* [Tsubouchi Shōyo and Futabatei Shimei collection]. Edited by Togawa Shinsuke and Aoki Toshihiro. Tokyo: Iwanami Shoten, 2002.

Tsukakoshi Kazuo. "Danjo dōkenron to joken shōsetsu" [Equal rights and women's rights fiction]. *Kokubungaku kenkyū* [Research in national literature] 57, no. 10 (1975): 13–20.

Tsunoda Bun'ei. *Nihon no joseimei: Rekishiteki tenbō* [Women's names in Japan: A historical view]. 3 vols. Tokyo: Kyoikusha, 1980–88.

Uchida Roan. "Josensei" [Female teacher]. In *Ikamono* [Imposter], 75–128. Tokyo: Kanao Bun'endō, 1909.

Utsunomiya Takako. *Joshi kanbun tokuhon.* Vol. 4. Tokyo: Keigyōsha, 1899.

Uzaki Rojo. *Tori no medama* [Bird's eye]. Tokyo: Koseikan Shoten, 1915.

von Mohl, Ottmar. *Doitsu kizoku no Meiji kyūteiki.* Translated by Kanamori Shigenari. Tokyo: Shinjinbutsuōraisha, 1988.

Wada Shigejirō. "Nakajima Shōen 'Sankan no meika' oboegaki" [Notes on Nakajima Shōen's "Noble flowers of the mountains"]. *Ritsumeikan bungaku* [Ritsumeikan literature] 10, no. 1 (1981): 435–36.

Wakakuwa Midori. *Kōgō no shōzō: Shōken Kōtaigō no kyōshō to josei no kokuminka* [The portrait of the empress: Representations of the empress dowager Shōken and the nationalization of women]. Tokyo: Chikuma Shobo, 2001.

"Wasei Raspuchin: Iino Kichisaburō to Shimoda Utako." *Shinchō* 45, no. 282 (2005): 34–37.

Yamaguchi Teitarō. *Meiji Kōgō* [The Meiji empress]. Tokyo: Nanbokusha, 1914.

Yamakawa Kikue. *Onna nidai no ki* [A record of two generations of women]. Tokyo: Heibonsha, 1972.

Yamakawa Michiko. *Jokan* [Imperial court woman]. Tokyo: Jitsugyō no Nihonsha, 1960.

Yamamoto Hiroo. *Yōfu Shimoda Utako: Heimin shimbun yori* [Vamp Shimoda Utako: From *Heimin shimbun*]. Nagoya: Fubaisha, 1999.

Yamamoto Matori. *Sei to bunka* = Gender/Sex/Sexuality, Culture. Tokyo: Hōsei Daigaku Shuppankyoku, 2004.

Yanagida Izumi. *Jiyūtō to seiji shōsetsu* [The Liberal Party and political novels]. Tokyo: Tokyo kōenkai, 1932.

Yanagida Izumi. *Seiji shōsetsu kenkyū* [Studies in political novels]. Tokyo: Shunjūsha, 1935.

Yayoshi Mitsunaga. *Meiji ishin go no shuppan: Honyakusho to seiji shōsetsu* [Publishing after the Meiji Restoration: Translated works and political novels]. N.p., 1987.

Yi Sunshin. "'Josensei' to Shimoda Utako: 'Daraku jogakusei' no hyōshō, moderu mondai o megutte" ['Female teacher' and Shimoda Utako: Examining issues of representations of 'degenerate schoolgirls' and the use of a prototype]. In *Honyaku no ken'iki: Bunka, shokuminchi, aidentiti* [Boundaries of translation: Culture, colony, and identity], edited by Tsukuba Daigaku Bunka Hihyō Kenkyūkai, 153–73. Tokyo: Isebu, 2004.

Yokozawa Kiyoko. *Jiyū minkenka Nakajima Nobuyuki to Kishida Toshiko: Jiyū e no tatakai* [Freedom and People's Rights Movement activists Nakajima Nobuyuki and Kishida Toshiko: The struggle toward freedom]. Tokyo: Akashi Shoten, 2006.

Yokozawa Kiyoko. "Kishida Toshiko shōron: Jidai no nakade" [An essay on Kishida Toshiko: Throughout the ages]. *Senshū shigaku* 30 (March 1999): 56–82.

Zi Xia [Shika; Bu Shang]. *Girei sōfuku shika den* [Zi Xia's narrative of ritual clothing and funerals]. Vols. 1–3 of *Raiki* [Sacred books], edited by Ichihara Kōkichi, Imai Kiyoshi, and Suzuki Ryūichi. Tokyo: Shūeisha, 1976.

English Sources

Anderson, Marnie S. *A Woman's Place: Gender, Politics, and the State in Meiji Japan*. Ann Arbor: University of Michigan Press, 2005.

Anderson, Marnie S. "Kishida Toshiko and the Rise of the Female Speaker in Meiji Japan," *U.S.-Japan Women's Journal* no. 30/31 (2006): 36–59.

Austin, J. L. *How to Do Things with Words*. Edited by J. O. Urmson and Marina Sbisà. 2d ed. Cambridge, MA: Harvard University Press, 2003.

Bal, Mieke. *Narratology: Introduction to the Theory of Narrative*. Toronto: University of Toronto Press, 1985.

Bardsley, Jan. "The New Woman Exposed: Redefining Women in Modern Japanese Photography." In *New Woman International: Representations in Photography and Film from the 1870s through the 1960s*, edited by Elizabeth Otto and Vanessa Rocco, 38–54. Ann Arbor: University of Michigan Press, 2011.

Bernstein, Gail Lee, ed. *Recreating Japanese Women, 1600–1945*. Berkeley: University of California Press, 1991.

Bourdaghs, Michael K. *The Dawn That Never Comes: Shimazaki Tōson and Japanese Nationalism*. New York: Columbia University Press, 2003.

Bowen, Roger W. *Rebellion and Democracy in Meiji Japan: A Study of Commoners in the Popular Rights Movement*. Berkeley: University of California Press, 1980.

Bronner, Stephen Eric, and Douglas Kellner. *Critical Theory and Society: A Reader*. New York: Routledge, 1989.

Butler, Judith. *Excitable Speech: A Politics of the Performative*. New York: Routledge, 1997.

Butler, Judith. *Gender Trouble: Feminism and the Subversion of Identity*. New York: Routledge, 2006.

Cohn, Dorrit. *Transparent Minds: Narrative Modes for Presenting Consciousness in Fiction*. Princeton, NJ: Princeton University Press, 1978.

Copeland, Rebecca L. *Lost Leaves: Women Writers of Meiji Japan*. Honolulu: University of Hawai'i Press, 2000.

Copeland, Rebecca L., and Melek Ortabasi, eds. *The Modern Murasaki: Writing by Women of Meiji Japan*. New York: Columbia University Press, 2006.

Czarnecki, Melanie. "Bad Girls from Good Families: The Degenerate Meiji Schoolgirl." In *Bad Girls of Japan*, edited by Laura Miller and Jan Bardsley, 49–64. New York: Palgrave Macmillan, 2005.

Danly, Robert Lyons, and Ichiyō Higuchi. *In the Shade of Spring Leaves: The Life and Writings of Higuchi Ichiyō, a Woman of Letters in Meiji Japan*. New Haven, CT: Yale University Press, 1981.

De Bary, William Theodore, Yoshiko Kurata Dykstra, William M. Bodiford, J. S. A. Elisonas, and Philip B. Yampolsky. *Sources of Japanese Tradition*. 2 vols. New York: Columbia University Press, 2001.

De Lange, William. *A History of Japanese Journalism: Japan's Press Club as the Last Obstacle to a Mature Press*. Richmond, England: Japan Library, 1998.

Duke, Benjamin C. *The History of Modern Japanese Education: Constructing the National School System, 1872–1890*. New Brunswick, NJ: Rutgers University Press, 2009.

Ehrlich, Susan. *Representing Rape: Language and Sexual Consent*. London: Routledge, 2001.

Ericson, Steven J. *The Sound of the Whistle: Railroads and the State in Meiji Japan*. Cambridge, MA: Council on East Asian Studies, Harvard University, 1996.

Felman, Shoshana. *The Scandal of the Speaking Body: Don Juan with J. L. Austin, or Seduction in Two Languages*. Stanford, CA: Stanford University Press, 2003.

Fogel, Joshua A. "Kano Naoki's Relationship to Kangaku." In *New Directions in the Study of Meiji Japan*, edited by Adam L. Kern and Helen Hardacre, 358–72. Leiden, Netherlands: Brill, 1997.

Fraleigh, Matthew. "Songs of the Righteous Spirit: 'Men of High Purpose' and Their Chinese Poetry in Modern Japan." *Harvard Journal of Asiatic Studies* 69, no. 1 (2009): 109–71.

Friedman, Susan Stanford. "Women's Autobiographical Selves: Theory and Practice." In *Women, Autobiography, Theory: A Reader*, edited by Sidonie Smith and Julia Watson, 72–82. Madison: University of Wisconsin Press, 1998.

Fujitani, T. *Splendid Monarchy: Power and Pageantry in Modern Japan*. Berkeley: University of California Press, 1996.

Fukuzawa Yukichi. *The Autobiography of Fukuzawa Yukichi*. Translated by Eiichi Kiyooka. New York: Columbia University, 2007.

Gluck, Carol. *Japan's Modern Myths: Ideology in the Late Meiji Period*. Princeton, NJ: Princeton University Press, 1985.

Habermas, Jurgen. *Critical Theory and Society: A Reader*. Edited by Stephen Eric Bronner and Douglas M. Kellner. Translated by Sara Lennox and Frank Lennox. New York: Routledge, 1989.

Hane, Mikiso, trans. and ed. *Reflections on the Way to the Gallows: Rebel Women in Prewar Japan*. Berkeley: University of California Press, 1988.

Hastings, Sally A. "The Empress' New Clothes and Japanese Women, 1868–1912." *Historian* 55, no. 4 (1993): 677–92.

Hastings, Sally A. "Hatoyama Haruko: Ambitious Woman." In *The Human Tradition in Modern Japan*, edited by Anne Walthall, 81–98. Wilmington, DE: SR Books, 2002.

Hastings, Sally A. "Women Educators of the Meiji Era and the Making of Modern Japan." *International Journal of Social Education* 6, no. 1 (1991): 83–94.

Howland, Douglas. *Personal Liberty and Public Good: The Introduction of John Stuart Mill to Japan and China*. Toronto: University of Toronto Press, 2005.

Huffman, James L. *Creating a Public: People and Press in Meiji Japan*. Honolulu: University of Hawai'i Press, 1997.

Ishii, Ryōsuke. *Japanese Legislation in the Meiji Era*. Translated by William J. Chambliss. Tokyo: Pan-Pacific Press, 1958.

Judge, Joan. *The Precious Raft of History: The Past, the West, and the Woman Question in China*. Stanford, CA: Stanford University Press, 2008.

Kaikoku Hyakunen Kinen Bunka Jigyōkai. *A Cultural History of the Meiji Era*. Vol. 5. Tokyo: Pan-Pacific Press, 1958.

Kamei, Hideo. "The Transformability of Self-Consciousness: Fantasies of Self in the Political Novel." Translated by John Mertz. In *Transformations of Sensibility: The Phenomenology of Meiji Literature*, 23–42. Ann Arbor: University of Michigan Press, 2002.

Kano, Ayako. *Acting Like a Woman in Modern Japan: Theater, Gender and Nationalism*. New York: Palgrave Macmillan, 2001.

Karatani, Kojin. *Origins of Japanese Literature*. Durham, NC: Duke University Press, 1993.

Keene, Donald. *Emperor of Japan: Meiji and His World, 1852–1912*. New York: Columbia University Press, 2002.

Kishida Toshiko. "Daughters in Boxes." Translated by Rebecca L. Copeland and Aiko Okamoto MacPhail. In *The Modern Murasaki: Writing by Women of Meiji Japan*, edited by Rebecca L. Copeland and Melek Ortabasi, 62–71. New York: Columbia University Press, 2006.

Ko, Dorothy. *Teachers of the Inner Chambers: Women and Culture in Seventeenth-Century China*. Stanford, CA: Stanford University Press, 1994.

Ko, Dorothy, JaHyun Kim Haboush, and Joan R. Piggott, eds. "Introduction." In *Women and Confucian Cultures in Premodern China, Korea, and Japan*. Berkeley: University of California Press, 2003.

Kornicki, Peter Francis. *The Book in Japan: A Cultural History from the Beginnings to the Nineteenth Century*. Honolulu: University of Hawai'i Press, 2001.

Kornicki, P. K., Mara Patessio, and G. G. Rowley, eds. *The Female as Subject: Reading and Writing in Early Modern Japan*. Ann Arbor: Center for Japanese Studies, University of Michigan, 2010.

Koyama, Noboru. "Cultural Exchange at the Time of the Anglo-Japanese Alliance." In *The Anglo-Japanese Alliance, 1902–1922*, edited by Phillips Payson O'Brien, 203–6. London: RoutledgeCurzon, 2004.

Koyama, Shizuko. *Ryōsai Kenbo: The Educational Ideal of "Good Wife, Wise Mother" in Modern Japan*. Translated by Stephen Filler. Leiden, Netherlands: Brill, 2015.

Landes, Joan B. *Feminism, the Public and the Private*. New York: Oxford University Press, 1998.

Lebra, Takie Sugiyama. *Above the Clouds: Status Culture of the Modern Japanese Nobility*. Berkeley: University of California Press, 1995.

Lejeune, Philippe. "Autobiography in the Third Person." Translated by Annette Tomarken and Edward Tomarken. *New Literary History* 9, no. 1 (Autumn 1977): 27–50.

Lublin, Elizabeth Dorn. *Reforming Japan: The Woman's Christian Temperance Union in the Meiji Period*. Vancouver: University of British Columbia Press, 2010.

Mackie, Vera. *Creating Socialist Women in Japan: Gender, Labour and Activism, 1900–1937*. Cambridge: Cambridge University Press, 2002.

Maeda Ai. "From Communal Performance to Solitary Reading: The Rise of the Modern

Japanese Reader." In *Text and the City: Essays on Japanese Modernity*, translated and edited by James A. Fujii, 223–54. Durham, NC: Duke University Press, 2004.

Marran, Christine L. *Poison Woman: Figuring Female Transgression in Modern Japanese Culture*. Minneapolis: University of Minnesota Press, 2007.

Matsuda Wataru. *Japan and China: Mutual Representations in the Modern Era*. Translated by Joshua A. Fogel. London: Routledge, 2013.

Mehl, Margaret. *Private Academies of Chinese Learning in Meiji Japan: The Decline and Transformation of the* Kangaku Juku. Copenhagen: Nordic Institute of Asian Studies Press, 2003.

Mehl, Margaret. "Women Educators and the Confucian Tradition in Meiji Japan (1868–1912): Miwada Masako and Atomi Kakei." *Women's History Review* 10, no. 4 (2001): 579–602.

Mertz, John Pierre. *Novel Japan: Spaces of Nationhood in Early Meiji Narrative, 1870–88*. Ann Arbor: Center for Japanese Studies, University of Michigan, 2003.

Miller, S. J. "Japanese Shorthand and Sokkibon." *Monumenta Nipponica* 49, no. 4 (Winter 1994): 471–87.

Molony, Barbara. "The Quest for Women's Rights in Turn-of-the-Century Japan." In *Gendering Modern Japanese History*, edited by Barbara Molony and Katherine Uno, 463–92. Cambridge, MA: Harvard University Asia Center, 2005.

Molony, Barbara, and Kathleen S. Uno, eds. *Gendering Modern Japanese History*. Cambridge, MA: Harvard University Asia Center, 2005.

Mori Ōgai. *The Historical Fiction of Mori Ōgai*. Edited by David Dilworth and J. Thomas Rimer. Honolulu: University of Hawai'i Press, 1991.

Mostow, Joshua S. "Modern Constructions of *Tales of Ise*: Gender and Courtliness." In *Inventing the Classics: Modernity, National Identity, and Japanese Literature*, edited by Haruo Shirane and Tomi Suzuki, 96–119. Stanford, CA: Stanford University Press, 2000.

Nagase, Mari. "Women Writers of Chinese Poetry in Late-Edo Period Japan." PhD diss., University of British Columbia, 2007.

Najita, Tetsuo. *Visions of Virtue in Tokugawa Japan: The Kaitokudō Merchant Academy of Osaka*. Chicago: University of Chicago Press, 1987.

Nolte, Sharon H., and Sally Ann Hastings. "The Meiji State's Policy Toward Women, 1890–1910." In *Recreating Japanese Women, 1600–1945*, edited by Gail Lee Bernstein, 151–74. Berkeley: University of California Press, 1991.

Ortabasi, Melek. "Tazawa Inabune (1874–1896)." In *The Modern Murasaki: Writing by Women of Meiji Japan*, edited by Rebecca L. Copeland and Melek Ortabasi, 151–60. New York: Columbia University Press, 2006.

Pateman, Carole. *The Disorder of Women: Democracy, Feminism, and Political Theory*. Stanford, CA: Stanford University Press, 1989.

Rodd, Laurel Rasplica. "Meiji Women's Poetry." In *The Modern Murasaki: Writing by Women of Meiji Japan*, edited by Rebecca L. Copeland and Melek Ortabasi, 29–33. New York: Columbia University Press, 2006.

Rowbotham, Sheila. *Woman's Consciousness, Man's World*. Harmondsworth, England: Penguin, 1973.

Sakaki, Atsuko. *Obsessions with the Sino-Japanese Polarity in Japanese Literature*. Honolulu: University of Hawai'i Press, 2006.

Sand, Jordan. *House and Home in Modern Japan: Architecture, Domestic Space, and Bourgeois Culture, 1880–1930*. Cambridge, MA: Harvard University Asia Center, 2005.

Schencking, J. Charles. "The Politics of Pragmatism and Pageantry: Selling a National Navy at the Elite and Local Level in Japan, 1890–1913." In *Nation and Nationalism in Japan*, edited by Sandra Wilson, 21–37. New York: Routledge, 2013.

Schneider, Helen M. *Keeping the Nation's House: Domestic Management and the Making of Modern China*. Vancouver: University of British Columbia Press, 2012.

Scott, Joan Wallach. "The Evidence of Experience." *Critical Inquiry* 17, no. 4 (Summer 1991): 773–97.

Scott, Joan Wallach. *Only Paradoxes to Offer: French Feminists and the Rights of Man*. Cambridge, MA: Harvard University Press, 1996.

Scott, Joan Wallach, and Debra Keates. *Going Public: Feminism and the Shifting Boundaries of the Private Sphere*. Urbana: University of Illinois Press, 2004.

Sekiguchi, Sumiko. "Confucian Morals and the Making of a 'Good Wife and Wise Mother': From 'Between Husband and Wife There Is Distinction' to 'As Husbands and Wives Be Harmonious.'" *Social Science Japan Journal* 13, no. 1 (2010): 95–113.

Sievers, Sharon. *Flowers in Salt: The Beginnings of Feminist Consciousness in Modern Japan*. Stanford, CA: Stanford University Press, 1983.

Smith, Sidonie, and Julia Watson. *Women, Autobiography, Theory: A Reader*. Madison: University of Wisconsin Press, 1998.

Suzuki Sadami. *The Concept of "Literature" in Japan*. Translated by Royall Tyler. Kyoto: International Research Center for Japanese Studies, 2006.

Suzuki, Tomi. "Gender and Genre: Modern Literary Histories and Women's Diary Literature." In *Inventing the Classics: Modernity, National Identity, and Japanese Literature*, edited by Tomi Suzuki and Haruo Shirane, 71–95. Stanford, CA: Stanford University Press, 2000.

Suzuki, Tomi. *Narrating the Self: Fictions of Japanese Modernity*. Stanford, CA: Stanford University Press, 1996.

Tanaka, Yukiko. *Women Writers of Meiji and Taishō Japan: Their Lives, Works and Critical Reception, 1868–1926*. Jefferson, NC: McFarland, 2000.

Tocco, Martha. "Made in Japan: Meiji Women's Education." In *Gendering Modern Japanese History*, edited by Barbara Molony and Katherine Uno, 39–60. Cambridge, MA: Harvard University Asia Center, 2005.

Tocco, Martha. "Norms and Texts for Women's Education in Tokugawa Japan." In *Women and Confucian Cultures in Premodern China, Korea, and Japan*, edited by Dorothy Ko, JaHyun Kim Haboush, and Joan R. Piggott, 193–218. Berkeley: University of California Press, 2003.

Tomasi, Massimiliano. *Rhetoric in Modern Japan: Western Influences on the Development of Narrative and Oratorical Style*. Honolulu: University of Hawai'i Press, 2004.

Tomida, Hiroko. *Hiratsuka Raichō and Early Japanese Feminism*. Leiden, Netherlands: Brill, 2004.

Tsuda, Umeko. *The Attic Letters: Ume Tsuda's Correspondence to Her American Mother*. Edited by Yoshiko Furuki. New York: Weatherhill, 1991.

Tuck, Robert James. "The Poetry of Dialogue: Kanshi, Haiku and Media in Meiji Japan, 1870–1900." PhD diss., Columbia University, 2012.

van Compernolle, Timothy. *The Uses of Memory: The Critique of Modernity in the Fiction of Higuchi Ichiyō*. Cambridge, MA: Harvard University Asia Center, 2006.

Voloshinov, V. N. *Marxism and the Philosophy of Language*. New York: Seminar Press, 1973.

INDEX

Printed and bound by CPI Group (UK) Ltd, Croydon, CR0 4YY

09/06/2025

14685674-0003